Presented to

....

From

....

On this date

....

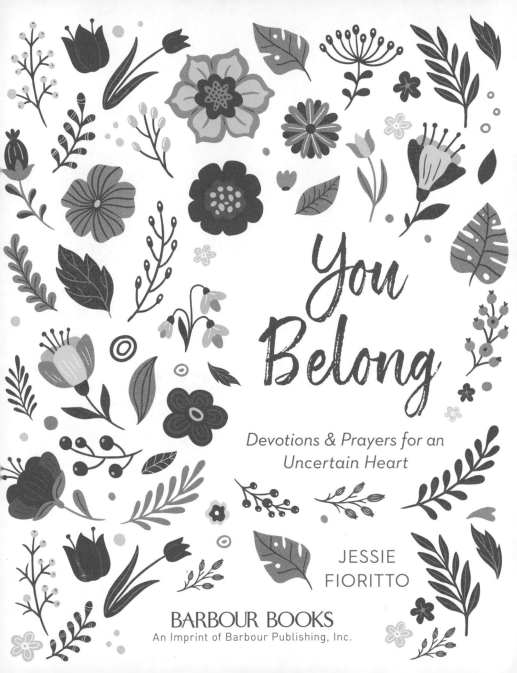

You Belong

Devotions & Prayers for an Uncertain Heart

JESSIE
FIORITTO

BARBOUR BOOKS
An Imprint of Barbour Publishing, Inc.

Published by Barbour Books, an imprint of Barbour Publishing, Inc., 1810 Barbour Drive, Uhrichsville, Ohio 44683, www.barbourbooks.com

Our mission is to inspire the world with the life-changing message of the Bible.

Member of the
Evangelical Christian
Publishers Association

Printed in China.

Introduction

Long before he laid down earth's foundations, he had us in mind, had settled on us as the focus of his love, to be made whole and holy by his love. Long, long ago he decided to adopt us into his family through Jesus Christ. (What pleasure he took in planning this!) He wanted us to enter into the celebration of his lavish gift-giving by the hand of his beloved Son. . . . He thought of everything, provided for everything we could possibly need, letting us in on the plans he took such delight in making.

EPHESIANS 1:4–6, 9 MSG

Your life is no cosmic accident, loved one. You are not here in this place at this time by chance. Your Father in heaven was thinking about you—yes, you—before He spoke this stunning universe into being. And, oh, the plans He has for you!

Don't be afraid to trust the One who knows your past and your future and loves you more deeply than you can imagine. He created you for a purpose, so step into His wonderful plans as He unveils the kingdom work He designed just for you on this earth. You'll discover how He satisfies every inner longing He placed in you with His abounding love, abundant grace, and abiding presence as you follow Him.

Experience the assurance of His promise to stay with you always, through both hardships and joys. You belong to Him. And right this minute He's preparing an exquisite, breathtaking eternal home for you—His beloved.

I'm His

GOD's Message, the God who made you in the first place,
Jacob, the One who got you started, Israel: "Don't be afraid, I've
redeemed you. I've called your name. You're mine. When you're in over
your head, I'll be there with you. When you're in rough waters, you will
not go down. When you're between a rock and a hard place, it won't
be a dead end—because I am GOD, your personal God, The Holy of
Israel, your Savior. I paid a huge price for you: all of Egypt, with rich
Cush and Seba thrown in! That's how much you mean to me!
That's how much I love you! I'd sell off the whole world
to get you back, trade the creation just for you.
ISAIAH 43:1–4 MSG

Sarah collapsed in tears. She'd scoured her house with the precision of a
CSI team, but she finally had to admit that the pearl earrings her mother
had given to her when she turned sixteen were gone. Her grandmother had
given those pearls to her mother. And her mother had given them to her.
Sarah's heart clenched in longing. She'd give anything to have them back.

God longs for you to be His with this same aching desire. You are a
precious daughter to Him, and He would trade the world for you—in fact,
He traded His Son.

*God, You bought me at a dear cost—the highest price—the life
of another given for me. Thank You that I am Yours. Amen.*

Planted by the River

His delight is in the law of the Lord, and on his law he meditates day and night. He is like a tree planted by streams of water that yields its fruit in its season, and its leaf does not wither.

PSALM 1:2–3 ESV

The landscape around you is dry and dusty. The arid wasteland seems unfit for growth, hostile toward new life. But in the midst of the devastation, a tree thrives. Its roots twine deeply into the soil beside a pool of water. New leaves unfurl on healthy green shoots. And its branches are heavy with succulent new fruit. You change direction and walk toward the promise of welcome refreshment. Oh, the relief of cool shade! You pluck a beautiful piece of fruit from its branches and deeply breathe in its sweet aroma. Your mouth waters as you bite into its juicy flesh. Heavenly!

You're called to be like that flourishing tree. God didn't plant you here in this world so you could prosper only for yourself; He planted you here to benefit all those around you. He asks you to draw from the life-giving water of His Word every day and thrive in this dried-up, dying world. The lost and suffering around you will be drawn to the fruit of your fellowship with the Holy Spirit—your love, joy, peace, patience, kindness, goodness, faithfulness, gentleness, and self-control will draw them toward the living water of Jesus that sustains you.

Lord, teach me to drink deeply of Your Word and thrive. Amen.

What a Girl Wants

*He withdrew from them about a stone's throw, and knelt down
and prayed, saying, "Father, if you are willing, remove this cup from me.
Nevertheless, not my will, but yours, be done." And there appeared
to him an angel from heaven, strengthening him.*

LUKE 22:41–43 ESV

"But, Mommy, I want to play on the swings! I do *not* want to take a nap!"
The little girl stomped her foot and crossed her arms as she huffed her
displeasure. Her angelic face and blond curls belied her dramatic temper
tantrum. But what she really needed, despite her desires, was some sleep!

Fast-forward to big-girl life. Have we really changed much from our
foot-stomping toddler selves? Or are we still digging our heels in and de-
manding our own way? Oh, you might not yell with theatrical flair (*usually*)
when you don't get your way, but does your prayer life reflect a total surrender to the One you belong to? When you pray, do you ask God only for
what you want, or do you ask Him what He wants for you?

Try it today. Tell God you're willing to forfeit your desires for His plans.
He loves you passionately, and He, in His great wisdom, knows just what
you need. Jesus was strengthened by an angel to carry out God's will. You
too can receive supernatural power to live God's way.

*Heavenly Father, help me unclench my fists and release my
selfish desires. My life is Yours. In Jesus' name, amen.*

Linger on Your Blessings

The LORD is my chosen portion and my cup; you hold my lot.
The lines have fallen for me in pleasant places; indeed,
I have a beautiful inheritance. I bless the LORD who gives
me counsel; in the night also my heart instructs me.

PSALM 16:5–7 ESV

David was not afraid to pour out his emotions openly to God—his pain and struggles and doubts. He dumped them out on God, who is big enough to handle our bigger-than-life emotions. But David didn't get hung up in that place of angst. After he purged his emotions, he fell back on the promises of God. He praised Him for who He is—faithful, good, loving, tender, and strong.

Remember to linger on your blessings, because Satan wants you to stay focused on your disappointments. But don't fall for the enemy's lies that God is not good, that He doesn't care, that He's abandoned us, that we deserve better and God has taken good things away from us.

What if, instead of focusing on our complaints, we looked to Jesus, anticipating and believing that at this very moment He is up to something good for us? Today, cultivate an anticipation for where and how you will spend millions of years in the presence of God—apart from the enemy, without pain and suffering. Because, friend, the lines have fallen in pleasant places for you!

Jesus, thank You for Your unimaginably good
plans for me, for my beautiful inheritance. Amen.

Not Too Flawed for Use

He said to me, "My grace is sufficient for you, for my power is made perfect in weakness." Therefore I will boast all the more gladly of my weaknesses, so that the power of Christ may rest upon me.

2 CORINTHIANS 12:9 ESV

"Mom, why do you hang on to this old cast-iron skillet?" Your daughter hefts the offending cookware from the stove and wrinkles her nose. "It looks terrible! Haven't you had it since God created woman or something? What you need is a brand-new, stainless pan, not this clunky chunk of metal."

Your skillet probably does seem flawed to her eyes. It *is* old. But what your daughter doesn't realize is that the chicken and roasted veggies she loves so much wouldn't taste quite so irresistible in another pan. The years of seasoning your cast-iron has undergone bring a unique flavor to the dish.

Have you doubted God's ability to use you because of your shortcomings? Throughout history God has been calling the faithless, the flawed, and the broken to do big things for Him. In spite of your weakness, He is strong. Through your failure, He is victorious. Trust that He can redeem every circumstance and past experience in your life for His purposes. Wait patiently for His timing, and see what He will do!

Heavenly Father, help me not to see my flaws as stumbling blocks, and give me patience as You season me for use in Your kingdom. Amen.

Bloom Where You're Planted

*"Build houses and live in them; plant gardens and eat their produce.
Take wives and have sons and daughters; take wives for your sons, and
give your daughters in marriage, that they may bear sons and daughters;
multiply there, and do not decrease. But seek the welfare of the city
where I have sent you into exile, and pray to the LORD on its
behalf, for in its welfare you will find your welfare."*

JEREMIAH 29:5–7 ESV

"When life hands you lemons, make lemonade." God may not have said these words, but it's exactly what He asked the Israelites to do during their exile in Babylon. Later in the chapter, He said, "I know the plans I have for you. . .plans to prosper you and not to harm you, plans to give you hope and a future" (Jeremiah 29:11 NIV). Can you imagine being carted off to slavery and God saying that He wants to prosper you? He was telling them to plan for their future in the face of their current hardship.

Jesus does the same for you. He enters your present circumstances and says that He wants you to dream here, to increase and not decrease, to be a blessing to those around you. Live today like you belong to the God of prosperity and hope! Whose life can you brighten as you go about the business of your day?

*Lord, You placed me right here and now. Show me how
to bless the people I see today. In Jesus' name, amen.*

Chosen

You are the ones chosen by God, chosen for the high calling of priestly work, chosen to be a holy people, God's instruments to do his work and speak out for him, to tell others of the night-and-day difference he made for you—from nothing to something, from rejected to accepted.

1 PETER 2:9–10 MSG

Who doesn't remember the angst-ridden childhood experience of waiting while the appointed team captains chose their teams? Everyone's nightmare of being picked last, or worse, not being picked at all, always seemed imminent. As humans we struggle with the insecurity of not belonging. Being left out. Uninvited. Unwanted.

Sometimes our lives here on this earth can fool us into thinking that our worst nightmare really has come true. But beware of listening to the lies the enemy would whisper into your ear. Satan would love to cut you off from God's truth. Even if the people who should love you best have rejected you, you are never unwanted. Because God has chosen you.

Yes, you with your freckles or too-loud laugh or social awkwardness or whatever flaw you despise about yourself. You have been singled out and gently led into God's marvelous light of acceptance. He has a high calling for the life He designed you to live. And only you can live it as He planned.

Father in heaven, I'm so grateful that I never have to fear rejection from You. You love me better than any other. Amen.

Glorious Living

It's in Christ that we find out who we are and what we are living for.
Long before we first heard of Christ and got our hopes up, he had
his eye on us, had designs on us for glorious living, part of the
overall purpose he is working out in everything and everyone.

EPHESIANS 1:11–12 MSG

Lizzy tapped her finger impatiently on her desk. The glowing circle on her computer screen kept spinning around and around. Around and around. She was tired of waiting for something to happen so she could get on with her work.

Have you been living your life in a holding pattern? Are you waiting to discover God's greater purpose for your life, or worse, assuming you have none? Precious daughter of God, you were created with a purpose. God planned with skill and great attention to detail all the good works He intended for you to accomplish. Don't be distressed if you're living a garden-variety life—no earth-shattering fame or world-changing discovery in sight. What if your purpose is to simply love the next person that you meet? Or to encourage your husband? Or to raise your children in the way that they should go?

Wake up from your waiting! Today is the day that God has given you to do His work.

Lord, thank You for the designs You have on my life.
Help me to embrace each moment and walk in Your
Spirit every step I take. In Jesus' name, amen.

Eternally His

*Then I saw a new heaven and a new earth, for the first heaven
and the first earth had passed away, and the sea was no more.
And I saw the holy city, new Jerusalem, coming down out of heaven
from God, prepared as a bride adorned for her husband. And I heard
a loud voice from the throne saying, "Behold, the dwelling place of
God is with man. He will dwell with them, and they will be his
people, and God himself will be with them as their God."*
REVELATION 21:1–3 ESV

A new mother cuddles her swaddled newborn against her chest, a precious little life she gave birth to. The bassinet stands empty beside her rocker because she'd much rather feel the slow rise and fall of her baby's tiny chest and caress the rose-petal skin against her cheek than put her little one away from her. Tiny fingers grasp her own, and she hopes never to be separated from her tiny bundle of happiness.

If you've never been embraced by the absolute love of an earthly parent, know that your heavenly Father adores you with openhearted devotion. He strolled in the garden with His first children, the masterpieces of His creation, and He also longs for your presence. His love for you is so great that He carefully crafted His plan so that you could join Him in eternity—never again to be parted.

Thank You, Jesus, for an eternal home with You. Amen.

God of the Impossible

*Your way, O God, is holy. What god is great like our God?
You are the God who works wonders; you have made known
your might among the peoples. You with your arm redeemed your
people, the children of Jacob and Joseph. When the waters saw you,
O God, when the waters saw you, they were afraid; indeed, the deep
trembled. The clouds poured out water; the skies gave forth thunder;
your arrows flashed on every side. The crash of your thunder was
in the whirlwind; your lightnings lighted up the world; the earth
trembled and shook. Your way was through the sea, your path
through the great waters; yet your footprints were unseen.
You led your people like a flock by the hand of Moses and Aaron.*
PSALM 77:13–20 ESV

What worries for this day could possibly be bigger than our majestic and powerful God? Trapped against the Red Sea, the Israelites waited for Pharaoh's chariots to overtake them. Fear hijacked their emotions, and they could not see their escape. All hope vanished. But we belong to a mighty God who makes paths through great waters! He provides when our human eyes see only impossibility. Trust in Him today for the way through your troubles.

Lord, You alone work wonders in my life. Thank You for miraculous solutions. And even if I am not delivered from my trials, I know You will strengthen me with endurance to persevere. In Jesus' name, amen.

Reclaimed

Therefore, if anyone is in Christ, he is a new creation. The old has passed away; behold, the new has come. All this is from God, who through Christ reconciled us to himself and gave us the ministry of reconciliation; that is, in Christ God was reconciling the world to himself, not counting their trespasses against them.

2 CORINTHIANS 5:17–19 ESV

The barn was one swift kick away from collapsing. It was a century old if it was a day, and its ridgeline sagged like a swaybacked mare. It listed distressingly far to the left—a major safety hazard, no doubt about it. But Anna saw opportunity in that heap of weathered wood. She gently pried off some of the siding and boards and stacked the lumber in the bed of her pickup. Back in her shop, she cleaned and planed the boards, cut off the rotten ends, and began building something new. As she glued and screwed the freshly shaped pieces together, a beautiful table emerged.

God can work this same regenerative creativity in your life. He can gather up all your broken pieces—the shards of your messed-up family, abuse, selfishness, loneliness, bitterness, and anger—and remake fresh your life that's breaking apart. He will give you a new purpose in Him and reconcile you to Him, the God who loves you. Come to Jesus. He will reclaim you from this world of sin.

Heavenly Father, I'm not broken anymore!
You've taken me back and remade me in Jesus! Amen.

Made for a Better Place

....

*God has made everything beautiful for its own time. He has
planted eternity in the human heart, but even so, people cannot
see the whole scope of God's work from beginning to end.*

ECCLESIASTES 3:11 NLT

Julie pulled open the refrigerator door and stared at its contents—again. She pushed the doors closed and moved to the pantry. Her gaze roved the shelves and dissected the box labels, but she saw nothing that would satisfy her particular hunger. She walked slowly away from the kitchen, her appetite longing for an elusive something that wasn't there.

Your heavenly Father planted eternity in your heart. He lovingly kissed your soul with a yearning for Him so that you would never be satisfied with less. C. S. Lewis wrote, "If I find in myself a desire which no experience in this world can satisfy, the most probable explanation is that I was made for another world."[1] Beloved of God, you were created for eternity. The ache you feel is homesickness—the desire for that breathtaking, everlasting land where the pain of this world will ebb in the radiance of God's glory. A place where goodbye is but a memory and sin is no more.

....

*God, thank You for the gnawing sense that there is something
more out there than this fleeting life. Forgive me for when I try to
live and move and be without You. In Jesus' precious name, amen.*

---

[1] C. S. Lewis, *Mere Christianity*, in *The Complete C. S. Lewis Signature Classics* (New York: HarperOne, 2002), 114.

Run for Him

But for this purpose I have raised you up, to show you my power,
so that my name may be proclaimed in all the earth.

EXODUS 9:16 ESV

Eric Liddell, the Flying Scotsman, won the gold medal in the 400-meter race at the 1924 Paris Olympic games. He refused to run in the heat for his favored 100 meters because it was held on a Sunday. He broke both the Olympic and world records with a time of 47.6 seconds. Liddell said, "I believe God made me for a purpose. . .but he also made me fast! And when I run I feel his pleasure."[2] Liddell then went on to serve as a missionary in China. He lived to bring God glory and to serve others.

You too were made for a purpose! God inscribed your passions into the fibers of your soul when He knit you together in the womb. You bring Him glory when you take up those passions and use them for His kingdom. He is delighted when you run with perseverance the race He has given you.

What makes you feel complete? Take that today and ask God what He would have you do with it, and feel His smile of approval.

Lord, I give You my passions and my plans.
Use me for Your glory. Amen.

---

[2] *Chariots of Fire*, directed by Hugh Hudson (Los Angeles: Twentieth Century Fox, 1981), DVD.

Only Good Gifts

Whatever is good and perfect is a gift coming down to us from God our Father, who created all the lights in the heavens. He never changes or casts a shifting shadow. He chose to give birth to us by giving us his true word. And we, out of all creation, became his prized possession.

JAMES 1:17–18 NLT

A little girl skipped among the swaying wildflowers, bending low to catch their sweet scent on the breeze. The forest glade was an unexpected serendipity during her afternoon explorations. The cheerful sunlight bathed the meadow in a warm glow. Peace enveloped her in her blooming paradise. But as evening approached, the shadows began to crawl out from the tree roots as the sun slinked toward the horizon. As their dark fingers stretched toward her, a trickle of unease skated down her spine.

Our perspective can often change when we see things in a different light. Activities that once seemed pleasurable and beneficial can often have dark side effects. That time we spend on social media can lead to toxic comparison and discontentment. That girl time with a friend may spiral into harsh gossip. Or that glossy red car could come with a monthly payment that strains your bank account. But we can live free of fear that God's gifts are anything but good. For He remains unchanged through the ages. He never casts a shifting shadow. And He has chosen to shower His goodness on you, His cherished possession.

*Heavenly Father, thank You for
Your rock-solid unchangeability. Amen.*

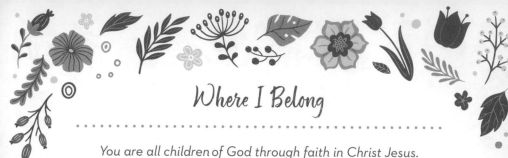

Where I Belong

*You are all children of God through faith in Christ Jesus.
And all who have been united with Christ in baptism have
put on Christ, like putting on new clothes. . . . And now that
you belong to Christ, you are the true children of Abraham.
You are his heirs, and God's promise to Abraham belongs to you.*
GALATIANS 3:26–27, 29 NLT

Chelsea had never had a family. She'd spent the first seven years of her life shuffling from one foster home to another. She had an ache deep in her chest to feel a mother's gentle caresses and to be squeezed in a father's hugs. Mostly she wanted someone to love her just because, no matter what. She wanted a place to belong.

Some of us come from families brimming with love and laughter while others' families are fraught with discord and tension. And some of us have no relatives at all. Unfortunately we can't browse the world with a shopping cart and select our family like we do our favorite fruit from the supermarket, but we *can* choose God's!

Whether your earthly family is wonderful, lacking, or nonexistent, you gain a whole slew of new siblings through your faith in Jesus. And you become God's child, a daughter showered with unconditional love and acceptance—not to mention an unimaginably fantastic inheritance waiting for you in heaven.

*Heavenly Father, thank You for
adopting me into Your family. Amen.*

My Forever Home

But there's far more to life for us. We're citizens of high heaven!
We're waiting the arrival of the Savior, the Master, Jesus Christ,
who will transform our earthy bodies into glorious bodies like his own.
He'll make us beautiful and whole with the same powerful skill by
which he is putting everything as it should be, under and around him.
PHILIPPIANS 3:20–21 MSG

The pain seems too great, the contractions too intense. Sweat rolls off of your trembling muscles, and you wonder if you will survive the labor. You wish that you could skip the trial and move right into the relief of delivery. And then with one last groan the pain ends. A baby's sharp cry breaks into the room. And your heart leaps in joy. A squirming bundle is placed on your chest, and you hope the moment never ends.

Friend, the struggles of this world are only temporary. Your true life is in heaven. We await its arrival with the same hopeful expectation of a mother-to-be. And when we enter its glorious perfection, the pains of this place will fade. Surely we'll be thinking, *I'm so glad that's over, and look what I have now!* We'll have, well, an eternity to enjoy the place where we belong.

Lord, strengthen me as I suffer through the pains of this
life right now, for You have promised that my homeland
is heaven! My experience there will so far surpass anything
I've known in this place! In Jesus' name, amen.

His Comforting Presence

So do not fear, for I am with you; do not be dismayed,
for I am your God. I will strengthen you and help you;
I will uphold you with my righteous right hand.

ISAIAH 41:10 NIV

"Will you come with me?" Pleading blue eyes meet yours as you look down at your frightened child perched on the top stair. Of course the basement seems intimidating to a four-year-old. It's cold and dark and cluttered with heaps of storage boxes that could hide all manner of big scary things. So you grasp her chubby fingers, flip on the light switch, and say, "Come on, pumpkin. Mommy will be right here beside you."

As mature, sophisticated women, we would never scurry a little faster across that same basement after dark, right? But we do encounter lonely and scary places that can leave us feeling vulnerable and small—the loss of a job, the death of a spouse, an illness. And God promises to take your hand and wade into these deep waters with you. Are you trusting His strength to sustain you, or are you doubting His presence in your troubling circumstances? Don't waste another second on worry. Grab on to this truth today: God is with you!

Heavenly Father, the enemy whispers that I'm
all alone. But I know the truth. In Your presence
I am never alone. In Jesus' name, amen.

Seen

Thereafter, Hagar used another name to refer to the Lord, who had spoken to her. She said, "You are the God who sees me."

Genesis 16:13 NLT

Evelyn sat on her bathroom floor, her chin resting on her knees as tears soaked her jeans. She felt like an outcast. Nasty rumors had been circulating on social media about her. Her so-called friends had moved on now to the newest gossip-worthy morsel, leaving her shredded by their vicious wit. Her parents were preoccupied with their jobs, and her siblings were every bit as self-absorbed as she had recently been. Did anyone really see her? Was everyone so unconcerned by her pain? Did no one care?

When the people closest to us are either spewing hurtful words or are so distracted that they seem blind to our existence, we can buy into the illusion that we are isolated and unlovable. But that lie comes straight from the deceptive tongue of the enemy. Beloved daughter, the truth is that you belong to a mighty yet gentle and tender Father in heaven. He is a God who sees you and every triumph and mishap and scratch and dent along the way. He misses nothing. And He cares deeply about you. He promises that if you seek Him you will find Him. Ask Him to show you all the ways He is holding you now, and then look with spiritual eyes and you will discover His gentle care for you.

Lord God, thank You for seeing me. Amen.

Just Like Jesus

*Therefore be imitators of God, as beloved children.
And walk in love, as Christ loved us and gave himself
up for us, a fragrant offering and sacrifice to God.*
EPHESIANS 5:1–2 ESV

Your older daughter runs to her crying sister and rubs circles on her back. "It's okay, peanut," she says. "You'll be just fine." She sounds exactly like you! And she's doing for her sister exactly what you did for her only a few moments ago. Kids are masterful at imitation. So much so that you also notice she's picked up some of your not-so-desirable habits too! But kids aren't the only experts at mimicry. Many of us adults are equally willing to do just about anything to be more like those we idolize, whether it's wearing the right clothes, living in the right neighborhood, or having the right job.

It's natural for children to want to be just like their parents when they're young. But who are you trying to follow? You are God's beloved child. Are you imitating His good character or looking to your fellow fallen humans for guidance and approval? Are you becoming more merciful, kind, generous, good, joyful, and humble? Are you emulating the sacrificial love of Jesus?

Father, I don't want to merely pay lip service to You. I don't want to follow rules without having an inner change. Make me more like You, Jesus. Show me when I am only wearing a mask of love. Amen.

Home in His Love

"I've loved you the way my Father has loved me. Make yourselves at home in my love. If you keep my commands, you'll remain intimately at home in my love. That's what I've done—kept my Father's commands and made myself at home in his love."
JOHN 15:9–10 MSG

Kate hurries up the sidewalk to her friend's door. Her spirits lift just seeing the wreath of spring flowers hanging there. As soon as she enters, her friend offers her every comfort—a hot mug of coffee, a cozy spot on the couch, and attentive conversation as they each share their burdens and joys. Her friend's love makes the difficult times somehow easier to bear. She truly has a gift for making others feel right at home. Kate wishes she could stay forever.

Jesus too wants you to make yourself at home in His love. Come right in to stay. Get comfortable, put your feet up, and share everything with Him. He will treat you so well that you will know how to truly love others. Obedience is the key to remaining in His great love. "If you keep my commands, you will remain in my love, just as I have kept my Father's commands and remain in his love" (John 15:10 NIV). So regardless of what struggles you encounter today, conquer them from a place of rest in God's love.

Father, I want to remain in Your love forever. Help me to view my whole life through the lens of Your love. Amen.

Keep Eternity in Mind

*"I am coming soon. Hold fast what you have,
so that no one may seize your crown."*
REVELATION 3:11 ESV

A warrior returns from battle a hero. People line the streets to welcome him. The intense cheering pushes him onward toward home. His sword hangs at his side, and his armor is battle scarred. He waves to the people he fought for—loved ones and friends in the crowd. When he reaches his home, he sees his father waiting for him in front of the house. A big smile creases his father's face. He steps forward and pulls his son into a tight hug. "Well done, my son. Well done, indeed. Welcome home."

Have you thought about what your homecoming into the kingdom might look like? Do you consider eternity at all as you go through the motions of your day? Beloved, our lives here are not without purpose. Someday you're going to be received into God's presence and welcomed to your forever home. What do you want that day to look like? Your labors, victories, and faithfulness today will determine your reception. Stay the course, soldier, to make it a joyous arrival!

*Father, I'm coming home someday! Give me courage under
fire in this battle zone. I can't wait to finally enter Your presence
and find rest from this war. I want so badly to hear You say,
"Well done, My daughter!" In Jesus' name, amen.*

The Sting of Judgment

*So there is now no condemnation awaiting those who belong
to Christ Jesus. For the power of the life-giving Spirit—
and this power is mine through Christ Jesus—has freed
me from the vicious circle of sin and death.*

ROMANS 8:1–2 TLB

You slide into a chair opposite your friend at your favorite coffee shop. It's been awhile since you were able to find time in both your busy schedules. The tantalizing aroma of a designer brew wafts from your mug, and you feel the tension oozing from your muscles. This is *nice*. Girl time and coffee (with whipped cream and chocolate syrup, of course!), what could be more refreshing?

But then the conversation turns to the latest trouble you've been having with your daughter. And that's when you see it. The slight tightening around your friend's mouth. The slow up-tilt of her chin. The raised eyebrows. The judgment. Without a shred of empathy, she has evaluated and condemned your actions as less than satisfactory. Ah, now you remember why it's been so long since you last saw her. You slink from your chair with shame and regret as your new companions.

Friends, you can walk away from the unwanted company of guilt and shame. Make a new friend! Jesus offers encouragement and forgiveness instead of condemnation. And His death has destroyed sin's power.

*Jesus, thank You for freeing me. Empower me
by the Holy Spirit to walk in freedom. Amen.*

A Beautiful Spirit

Don't be concerned about the outward beauty of fancy hairstyles, expensive jewelry, or beautiful clothes. You should clothe yourselves instead with the beauty that comes from within, the unfading beauty of a gentle and quiet spirit, which is so precious to God.

1 PETER 3:3–4 NLT

The oleander's showy, funnel-shaped blooms are a gardener's gorgeous dream, but ingesting even a single leaf can be fatal. Even the smoke from burning oleander wood is toxic, and the milky sap can leave your skin itchy and irritated. This plant definitely possesses a prickly personality. But despite its poisonous nature, many still plant this ornamental shrub in their flower beds and feast their eyes on its beauty.

As women we often have a fascination for pretty wrapping, including our own. New clothes, a trendy haircut, and maybe a pedicure are just what the doctor ordered when we're feeling a little frumpy. But it's our spirits that are precious to God. A beautiful outside matters little to God if we're spewing poison from within. His desire for us is not flawless skin and a golden tan but rather the unfading radiance of a quiet and gentle spirit—a heart turned toward Him that chooses trust over panic and tenderness over harsh words.

Father, teach me gentleness for those I encounter. Whether it's my upset child or a difficult acquaintance, may my response be beautiful in Your eyes. Amen.

Tears in a Bottle

You keep track of all my sorrows. You have collected all my tears in your bottle. You have recorded each one in your book.

PSALM 56:8 NLT

In the movie *Leap!* an orphan girl wanted to be a ballerina. But when she complained about the rigorous training, her instructor said, "It's when you're tired you start to progress."[3] And how true of our own walk with God. It's usually not until we reach the end of our own rope that we grab ahold of God's.

Our response to our trials is usually "I want out. Make it stop, God!" But we also know that delivery from our trials is not always His answer. Because God is less concerned with removing our problems than He is with who we become because of them. In her book *Fully Alive*, Susie Larson wrote: "Though I was after relief, God wanted me to have a reward for my faith. Though I longed for a break, He wanted me to have a breakthrough. Though my gaze often drifted toward my problems, God was training me to think of eternity."[4]

God is not blind to our pains here; they're real and they hurt. He sees every injury inflicted and records it for the day when He will return and everyone's truth will be told.

Heavenly Father, my persistence and pain don't go unnoticed by You. Your justice will reign in the end. Mold me into a usable instrument for Your kingdom. Amen.

---

[3] *Leap!*, directed by Eric Summer and Eric Warin (New York: The Weinstein Company, 2016), DVD.
[4] Susie Larson, *Fully Alive* (Grand Rapids: Bethany House Publishers, 2018).

Breathless Anticipation

*But as it is, they desire a better country, that is, a heavenly one.
Therefore God is not ashamed to be called their God,
for he has prepared for them a city.*

HEBREWS 11:16 ESV

God is eagerly anticipating the day He will take our breath away with what He's prepared for us in eternity. We can trust in His great goodness and boundless creativity to come up with something wonderfully perfect—exactly what we've been waiting for. Can't you just picture Jesus' excitement as He talked with His best friends before He ascended into heaven? "I'm going to get your new place ready, guys! It's going to be fantastic. I'll be back soon to get you, and I can't wait to show you around! Don't forget about me!"

Author John Burke wrote, "What if we became people who have a vision for the ultimate Life to come? What if it's true that this life is merely a tiny taste on the tip of our tongues of the feast of Life yet to come? What if Heaven is going to be better than your wildest dreams? And what if how you live really does matter for the Life to come? That would change how we live, work, love, sacrifice—wouldn't it?"[5]

*God, I can't wait for You to take my breath
away with my first glimpse of eternity. Amen.*

---

[5] John Burke, *Imagine Heaven: Near-Death Experiences, God's Promises, and the Exhilarating Future That Awaits You* (Grand Rapids: Baker Books, 2015), 30, Kindle.

Praise Him!

As for me, I will always have hope; I will praise you more and more.
My mouth will tell of your righteous deeds, of your saving acts
all day long—though I know not how to relate them all.

PSALM 71:14–15 NIV

Too often we're totally entangled in problems.

Worrying about our problems.

Discussing our problems.

Thinking about our problems.

Pointing out other people's problems.

Our destructive thoughts are stuck on replay, and we seem to have forgotten how great God is. We forget to tell Him how awesome He is because we're so distracted by worry that we fail to notice all the times He's taken care of us. Not to mention the problems He's prevented that we don't even know about!

Today choose praise over melancholy because, as the psalmist said, you always have hope! You are saved. You are redeemed. You are chosen. You are forgiven. You are loved so much! Depression and despair can't hang around in the face of praise. Spend the day being grateful to your Savior. Gratitude will lift your spirits and draw you closer to God. The more you notice all the little ways God cares for you, the deeper your love for Him will become.

Heavenly Father, I don't deserve any of this. What I really
deserve is punishment, but You shower me with blessings instead.
Thank You for caring about me, comforting me, saving me,
and providing for me in countless ways every day. Amen.

A Good Plan

"For I know the plans I have for you," says the LORD. "They are plans for good and not for disaster, to give you a future and a hope."

JEREMIAH 29:11 NLT

How would our perspective change if the condition of our souls were visible to the naked eye? Some would no doubt be luminous, bright, and attractive, while others would be shrouded in darkness and crisscrossed with chains. As Jesus followers our hope for something better than we have here—an everlasting future with God in the eternal sunshine of His glory—should be a brilliant beacon that woos others out of the darkness to ask, "Why does your hope burn so brightly?"

God has great plans for you. Better than that, He has amazing plans for you. His Word is filled with the hope of your bright future. But we also live in the fallen world of "not yet." That means we won't experience all His promises in this life. So we live on a diet of faith and hope, walking faithfully in this world while expectantly waiting for the next.

C. S. Lewis wrote, "It is since Christians have largely ceased to think of the other world that they have become so ineffective in this. Aim at Heaven and you will get earth 'thrown in.'"[6] Does the light of your soul attract others to Jesus?

God, thank You for Your good plans. Amen.

---

[6] C. S. Lewis, *Mere Christianity*, in *The Complete C. S. Lewis Signature Classics* (New York: HarperOne, 2002), 112.

Child of Promise

Therefore we do not lose heart. Though outwardly we are wasting away, yet inwardly we are being renewed day by day. For our light and momentary troubles are achieving for us an eternal glory that far outweighs them all. So we fix our eyes not on what is seen, but on what is unseen, since what is seen is temporary, but what is unseen is eternal.

2 CORINTHIANS 4:16–18 NIV

An old Kenny Rogers song called "The Greatest" tells of a little boy who's convinced he's the greatest baseball player ever. He throws his ball up and swings. The ball plops to the ground. So again he throws the ball in the air. Again it lands in the dirt at his feet. Instead of becoming discouraged, he closes his eyes and imagines the cheers of his fans. He tosses his ball up again—strike three. Is he discouraged? No! Instead he realizes he must be an all-star pitcher.

Are you a glass half-empty or a glass half-full type of person? Paul had the nerve to call our lives "light and momentary" troubles because he guarded his perspective. He realized that he belonged to a God of promises and hope. But God doesn't promise a struggle-free life. Do you need an overhaul today on how you talk about your trials in this not-yet world?

Lord, I am Yours, and I trust in Your good promises. Amen.

A Father's Love

"My son, do not regard lightly the discipline of the Lord, nor be weary when reproved by him. For the Lord disciplines the one he loves, and chastises every son whom he receives." It is for discipline that you have to endure. God is treating you as sons. For what son is there whom his father does not discipline? . . . He disciplines us for our good, that we may share his holiness. For the moment all discipline seems painful rather than pleasant, but later it yields the peaceful fruit of righteousness to those who have been trained by it.

<small>HEBREWS 12:5–7, 10–11 ESV</small>

Through discipline and the pain and sacrifice of daily training, marathon runners shape their bodies into strong and sculpted endurance machines. They avoid empty calories while feeding their bodies the best nutrients. They rest adequately and work out daily.

Satan would have you believe that God is punishing you or depriving you when you experience hard things in life. But the difference between discipline and punishment is in the intent. Punishment brings shame and pain, while discipline results in nurturing and training. God is not waiting to beat you with a stick when you mess up. Instead He's looking out for your good! He loves you greatly and wants you to share in His holiness and grow in maturity.

And the best part is that God's discipline in your life proves your adoption as His child!

Heavenly Father, may I always remember that You discipline those You love. Amen.

I'm with Him

"Don't be afraid!" Elisha told him. "For there are more on our side than on theirs!" Then Elisha prayed, "O LORD, open his eyes and let him see!" The Lord opened the young man's eyes, and when he looked up, he saw that the hillside around Elisha was filled with horses and chariots of fire.

2 KINGS 6:16–17 NLT

A lone soldier stands motionless, relaxed and unconcerned as his enemy attacks. Their warhorses churn up the sod, spraying clods of dirt behind them. The earth trembles with the force of their hammering hooves. Their faces are smeared in grotesque paint, and the sun flashes like lightning against the honed blades of their weapons. Yet the soldier remains still.

Then, just as it seems the enemy will sweep over him with barely a break in their stride, a silhouette crests the hill behind the soldier. And then another. And another—until an army of thousands now stands behind the warrior. The cavalry charge jerks to a standstill. With screams and snorts from their animals, they flee.

You are not alone, beloved. Just as God didn't abandon Elisha to his enemies, heavenly armies with supernatural powers stand behind you. Never fear in the face of terrifying spiritual attack. God promises if you resist the devil that he will have no recourse but to flee from you (see James 4:7).

Heavenly Father, give me the strength to resist Satan's attacks because I belong to the mighty army of the living God. Amen.

Sacred Moments

So here's what I want you to do, God helping you: Take your everyday, ordinary life—your sleeping, eating, going-to-work, and walking-around life—and place it before God as an offering.

ROMANS 12:1 MSG

Holding a glowing candle in a hushed midnight Christmas Eve service or rising at daybreak on Easter Sunday—these moments feel sacred, reverent, worshipful. But what about today? What about today's laundry pile and stacked-up dishes? Shopping for groceries and paying bills? Changing diapers and making dinner? Can these mundane activities be holy offerings to God as well?

Andrew Peterson wrote that "there are no unsacred moments; there are only sacred moments and moments we have forgotten are sacred. If that's true, then it is our duty to reclaim the sacredness of our lives, of life itself."[7]

Take back the minutes of your day. Reclaim them from the lie that nothing holy dwells in the many monotonous moments between your first blink of rising and your last sigh before sleep.

Approach each task with an attitude of prayer, seeking Him in each chore and knowing that you are exactly where you belong in this moment—exactly where He has placed you.

Lord, may I live each day, each hour, each minute for You.
Because each of my moments is part of Your story. Amen.

---

[7] Andrew Peterson, foreword to Douglas McKelvey, *Every Moment Holy* (Nashville, TN: Rabbit Room, 2017), xvii–xviii.

Saved by His Life

God shows his love for us in that while we were still sinners, Christ died for us. Since, therefore, we have now been justified by his blood, much more shall we be saved by him from the wrath of God. For if while we were enemies we were reconciled to God by the death of his Son, much more, now that we are reconciled, shall we be saved by his life.

ROMANS 5:8–10 ESV

Lightning streaks skeletal fingers across the sky in a dazzling flash. The world holds its breath for a beat. Then two. A boom of thunder echoes deep and powerful in the distance. The earth trembles. This furious display is followed by a gentle rain that waters and nourishes the tender shoots of spring.

We serve an awesome God who is capable of great power and demands justice from His wayward-hearted creations. Yet He withholds His wrath because He is also mercy—scandalous and unexpected mercy that is spurred on by a tender love.

God's thunderous display reminds of us His power, of our fearful position if we were to receive our due punishment. But then comes the gentle rain. He showers us with His mercy because of Jesus, who loves us and endured that storm of wrath for us—so that we could experience the life-giving rains of grace.

Thank You, Jesus. I cannot imagine what You endured on that cross when You became sin and the sole focus of God's mighty wrath. Thank You. Amen.

Real Life

He pointed out to me a river of pure Water of Life, clear as crystal, flowing from the throne of God and the Lamb, coursing down the center of the main street. On each side of the river grew Trees of Life, bearing twelve crops of fruit, with a fresh crop each month; the leaves were used for medicine to heal the nations. There shall be nothing in the city that is evil; for the throne of God and of the Lamb will be there, and his servants will worship him. And they shall see his face; and his name shall be written on their foreheads. And there will be no night there—no need for lamps or sun—for the Lord God will be their light; and they shall reign forever and ever.

REVELATION 22:1–5 TLB

Eternity. It's brain-teasingly hard to imagine what it will be like to live in God's heavenly city. We know that Jesus went to get our digs all spiffed up for us, and we know that we're supposed to anticipate the promise of this incredible place, but at the same time we're left wondering, *What exactly am I supposed to be so excited about?* We won't truly know until we arrive. But one thing is for sure, God is not inviting you to an endless, boring sermon. He's inviting you to real, beyond-your-imagination life!

Jesus, Thank You for the promise of new life. Show me how to live for You here and now in my everyday life. Amen.

Created for Kindness

If anyone forces you to go one mile,
go with him two miles.
MATTHEW 5:41 ESV

Robin was so exhausted. Life lately had been hard—downright difficult! And everyone around her seemed to be vacationing and traveling. Well, she wasn't going anywhere. In fact, she needed to go cook dinner for everyone else in the family before they started complaining about their grumbling tummies. She went into the kitchen and glanced at her phone. One of her friends had just posted a picture of her gorgeous room-service dinner. *Hmm. Where's my room service, Lord?* she wondered. A few minutes later her phone chimed again, this time with a text. She stared at her screen in total disbelief. Her friend was sending her a complete dinner for the next day. When the food arrived, Robin discovered not only dinner but a bottle of bath soap and a candle along with a note: *"Enjoy your free time."*

Do you have a friend who always makes you feel like somebody special? Most of the time we just float through our day being nice to the people we meet. We ask them how they're doing to be polite, yet we don't really care. But kindness reaches out to lighten someone's load. Kindness sees a burden and offers to carry it for a while. The kindness of Jesus is irresistibly attractive. How can you become more like the One you belong to today?

Jesus, show me someone today who
needs my act of kindness. Amen.

What's the Cost?

So that we would not be outwitted by Satan;
for we are not ignorant of his designs.
2 CORINTHIANS 2:11 ESV

Bethany smiles at her six-year-old's squeal of delight and sparkling eyes as she pirouettes around her new bike—with no training wheels! Her daughter caresses the cushioned seat, trails her fingers through the pink-and-white streamers, and rings the bell. "I can't wait to ride it, Mommy! Can I go right now? Please. Please. Pretty please!" But before the blessed event can happen, Bethany sits down with her daughter to spell out the rules for safe biking. "Your helmet protects you from serious head injuries. You must wear it every time you ride your bike. If you do not, you will lose your riding privileges for a week."

If only we could so clearly see the consequences for all of our choices. When we understand the price we'll pay for a poor choice, we make better ones! God has a good plan for your life, just as His Word promises. But Satan also has designs on you—and not for your benefit! Scripture says that he comes to steal and kill and destroy. When you face temptation this week, stop and ask yourself, *How much is this going to cost me?*

Heavenly Father, the plans You have for me are so much better
than a momentary pleasure that will leave me filled with guilt
and shame. Show me when I am being tempted. Amen.

The Brave Choice

*I eagerly expect and hope that I will in no way be ashamed,
but will have sufficient courage so that now as always Christ
will be exalted in my body, whether by life or by death.*
<small>PHILIPPIANS 1:20 NIV</small>

She was going to do it. Joan inhaled deeply and released a slow cleansing breath before she opened her car door. Today she was not going to hand over control of her emotions to Helen. That woman made everyone's day miserable with her criticism and rudeness. But today Joan gathered her courage to love her in spite of her meanness. Her choice would probably be wildly unpopular among her coworkers because their favorite break-room gossip always included Helen. But this time when she saw Helen stalking down the hall, the familiar snarl twisting her lips, Joan smiled back.

The good Samaritan is often touted for his compassion. He had the courage to show kindness to someone who probably didn't like him back, maybe even hated him because of cultural bigotry. Have you been faced with a situation like this recently, one where you've had to decide if you were going to do the right thing regardless of whether it was popular, applauded, or even noticed? Take courage! Make the right choice!

*Heavenly Father, guide me and lend me Your strength
through every choice I make today. May I remain
unstained by my decisions. In Jesus' name, amen.*

Cast Your Cares

Cast all your anxiety on him
because he cares for you.
1 PETER 5:7 NIV

Have you ever looked at other people and wondered, *Why am I so messed up? Why are my seams coming loose and my edges unraveling? Why does my anxiety flare over every minor hiccup in my day?*

I've been there too. So have most of us. Something small happens: your appointment gets canceled or your child takes this moment to stomp and yell his displeasure over your yogurt choice right there in the grocery aisle, and your heart begins to race and sweat pops out on your forehead. You feel your last thread of sanity pulling loose, and you grab for it—but miss.

There's hope for your anxious heart, sweet sister. It lies in trust. Cast all of your cares that are rooted in distrust and unbelief on Him. Your cares about your family. Your cares about your personal life. Your cares about work. Your cares for the present. Your cares for the future. Cast them all on the One whose shoulders really do carry the weight of the world. This burden is too heavy for you. Let it go. And trust God. Trust that He is big enough, wise enough, and powerful enough to take on your cares. He is enough.

Lord, I'm done trying to control everything. I give all my
fears to You. I trust You with the details of my life because
I don't want to worry about them anymore. Amen.

My True Country

"LORD, remind me how brief my time on earth will be. Remind me that my days are numbered—how fleeting my life is. . . ." We are merely moving shadows, and all our busy rushing ends in nothing. We heap up wealth, not knowing who will spend it. And so, Lord, where do I put my hope? My only hope is in you.

PSALM 39:4, 6–7 NLT

Lisa's feet hurt. She'd run out of gas on the hottest day of the year. Sweat trickled down her face as she trudged along the highway. She licked her dry lips. Ahead, a shimmering pool of water spilled across the roadway. Was her overheated mind playing tricks on her? They hadn't had rain in days. When she approached, she realized that the road was as scorched here as everywhere else. The image of water was merely a highway mirage.

The things of this earth are also a mirage or copy of what is to come. On our journey home, it's vital that we are neither unthankful for our blessings nor enthralled by them. C. S. Lewis wrote, "I must keep alive in myself the desire for my true country, which I shall not find till after death."[8]

The wrong perspective can lead you to empty pools of water. Be careful that you aren't seeking fulfillment, but instead pursue those things that have eternal value. Remember this life is short while eternity is long.

Father, renew my focus on heaven. Give me a new desire for things with eternal value. Amen.

---

[8] C. S. Lewis, *Mere Christianity*, in *The Complete C. S. Lewis Signature Classics* (New York: HarperOne, 2002), 114.

Handpicked

Jesus said to her, "Everyone who drinks of this water will be thirsty again, but whoever drinks of the water that I will give him will never be thirsty again. The water that I will give him will become in him a spring of water welling up to eternal life."

JOHN 4:13–14 ESV

Chloe hung her head, wishing she were invisible. Again. Her weight wasn't right. Her hair wasn't right. Her clothes were all wrong. And she wasn't pretty. Not like that woman on the treadmill across the gym. She had rock-solid abs and probably negative 2 percent body fat. Chloe sighed and retreated to the shower. She felt left out and lonely. Rejected. Less than. . .

Friend, have you ever battled the feeling that you don't measure up, that no one wanted you? Have you ever felt like an outcast, searching for a place of acceptance and belonging? Jesus met just such a woman beside a well. She was looking for fulfillment but dying of thirst for something much more satisfying than what she was getting. He offered her Himself. Never to thirst again for acceptance. Never to thirst again for love. He is the living water that fulfills our deepest longings.

Come to Jesus and drink of His message, and you will never again crave meaning from any other source. Not from friends or lovers. Not from the perfect number on a scale. Because God has handpicked you as His beloved daughter.

Lord, You have chosen me.
I will never thirst for another. Amen.

The Enemy's Plans

Be alert and of sober mind. Your enemy the devil prowls
around like a roaring lion looking for someone to devour.

1 PETER 5:8 NIV

Even if you don't live in Africa, beware, my friend—you're still in lion country. Your Father's enemy is now yours. And Satan is one vicious foe. He may have been defanged at Calvary, but he's got wicked claws. He knows you belong to Jesus. And he also knows that his defeat is already in the books. But he's one livid losing kitty. He doesn't just want to trip you up and slow you down either—he wants to devour you.

He's scheming right now to dangle desires in front of you that will make you want something that's outside of God's will for your life. If you are caught unaware by his traps, he will steal your joy, kill your hope, and destroy you. He's not above lying to you either. And the only way to fight back against his deception is with the truth. Read scripture daily, meditate on God's words, know His truth. Soak scripture into the fiber of your soul and wield it, like the razor-edged blade it is, to strike at your enemy. And the next time a hungry lion roars outside your tent, you can force him to turn tail and run with the powerful words of the almighty God.

God, You have chosen me. But walking with You also means being stalked
by a lion. Make me aware of his schemes. Give me wisdom and cunning.
Bring Your truth to my mind when I'm under attack. In Jesus' name, amen.

The Glow of Dawn

"You will tell his people how to find salvation through forgiveness of their sins. All this will be because the mercy of our God is very tender, and heaven's dawn is about to break upon us, to give light to those who sit in darkness and death's shadow, and to guide us to the path of peace."

LUKE 1:77–79 TLB

The waters of the Baltimore Harbor ran red with the glare of the rockets, and by the light of their explosions the American flag could be seen waving over Fort McHenry. Francis Scott Key was held captive aboard a ship in the harbor during the British bombardment of the fort. During the long dark night, Key waited with expectation for the morning light.

In the first ethereal glow of dawn, there's a flutter of movement over the fort. A flag snapped sharply in the brisk coastal breeze. He strained to see, but the darkness shrouded its colors. The glow on the horizon intensified. The sun's first crimson fingers stretched across the waters and painted the land in glorious amber light. His heavy spirit was buoyed in victory. The Star-Spangled Banner still waved!

The banner of Christ's victory over sin will never be lowered. You no longer have to tremble in the dark as you walk through this valley of the shadow of death. Heaven's dawn has broken! Salvation has come! His name is Jesus. And His mercy is tender.

Father, thank You for Your saving grace. Amen.

My Lighthouse

*Trust in the LORD with all your heart; do not depend
on your own understanding. Seek his will in all you do,
and he will show you which path to take.*

PROVERBS 3:5–6 NLT

The night was black as sin. Storm clouds had moved in unexpectedly and taken the captain unaware. Dark waves stretched angry fists to drag his ship to the murky ocean depths. But His greatest fear was the shallow coastal water and the nearby rocky shore. The screeching winds were approaching hurricane force, and he knew his ship was in danger of being splintered against the rocks. Disoriented by the storm and the lightless conditions, fear gripped him in its merciless fist. He no longer knew which direction would move him away from danger.

But then, through the wall of darkness, he saw a light, a blazing beacon through the storm. He wrestled his ship away from it and toward the open water. The captain praised God for the lighthouse and its keeper, who would never know of the lives he'd saved this night.

Friend, in this life it's going to rain. And it might not be a gentle spring drizzle. The winds might howl at you and threaten to break you apart on the jagged shores of illness, pain, loneliness, or poverty. But you belong to the Light. Hold on to your trust in Him with everything you've got, and He will lead you safely through.

Father, thank You for the guiding light of scripture. Amen.

His Very Own Possession

*The grace of God has appeared that offers salvation to all people.
It teaches us to say "No" to ungodliness and worldly passions,
and to live self-controlled, upright and godly lives in this present
age, while we wait for the blessed hope—the appearing of the glory
of our great God and Savior, Jesus Christ, who gave himself for
us to redeem us from all wickedness and to purify for himself
a people that are his very own, eager to do what is good.*

TITUS 2:11–14 NIV

"Oh, don't even ask Valerie. She won't come out with us anymore. She probably has to go feed a homeless person or read her Bible. Isn't that right, Val?"

Her friend's sharp sarcasm stung. She *had* changed since she started taking her faith in Jesus more seriously. And her friends didn't seem to understand her decisions lately. But she had gotten so fed up with the emptiness of her self-serving existence and had finally realized that Jesus had already redeemed her from that life. Now she was energized to do good things that pleased Him by helping others. She was excited to belong to Jesus! And she'd found joy in her new purpose by saying no to her sinful urges and yes to His will. And one day He would be coming back for her!

*God, You've trained me to live a new life, a holy life
that pleases You. I've thrown off my old sinful habits
because I've realized who I belong to! Amen.*

Surrender to His Will

"Abba, Father, all things are possible for you. Remove this cup from me. Yet not what I will, but what you will."

MARK 14:36 ESV

How could he have done this to you? His betrayal sliced up your insides like razor blades. He'd left you—for her. Why? His vague reasons left you feeling foolish and naive. You weren't available enough. She shared more of his interests. You thought your relationship was strong. Maybe not perfect, but things seemed smooth between you. And all the while he'd been seeing someone else.

Jesus understands betrayal. He's felt the sting of faithless friends and sellout loved ones. On the night before His crucifixion, Jesus washed Judas's feet and shared dinner with him, and then Judas sold him out for money. Later in the Garden of Gethsemane, while Jesus prayed through the hardest, most rock-bottom night in His life in preparation for a brutal death, all so His friends could be forgiven—His disciples fell asleep.

He gets it. Friends who've walked away. Spouses who've been unfaithful. Parents who've been abusive. When the ones who should love you the most reject you, He understands exactly how you feel. But He trusted God's plan. He forgave. And on the third day He rose!

Let go of the pain of your past. Welcome the growth it brought you. Allow the healing love of Jesus to wash over your rejection. And you too will rise!

God, not my will but Yours. I trust that
Your plan is good. In Jesus' name, amen.

My Rock

"I lay a stone in Zion, a tested stone, a precious cornerstone for a sure foundation; the one who relies on it will never be stricken with panic."

ISAIAH 28:16 NIV

I don't want to follow a weak God. I don't want to worship a powerless being. I want to strut right up to the enemy like David did to Goliath and shout, "I come to you in the name of the LORD of hosts, the God of the armies of Israel, whom you have defied. This day the LORD will deliver you into my hand" (1 Samuel 17:45–46 ESV).

We worship a God who is all. He reigns supreme. He absorbed everything this world threw at Him and came out the victor. This is our God. He plans for an eternity, not mere days.

Jesus confronted the Pharisees, saying " 'The stone that the builders rejected has become the cornerstone. . . .' And the one who falls on this stone will be broken to pieces; and when it falls on anyone, it will crush him" (Matthew 21:42, 44 ESV). Jesus is the solid, unmovable rock that we are built on. Your Jesus is no timid Savior. Anyone who comes against Him will break like glass.

When Your enemies seem to be looming large, read this passage and remember, *I'm with Him.*

Lord Jesus, what a mighty God I serve! The woes and fears of this world crash and shatter against You. What have I to fear? Amen.

Too Busy

"I will arise and go to my father, and I will say to him, 'Father, I have sinned against heaven and before you. I am no longer worthy to be called your son. Treat me as one of your hired servants.' And he arose and came to his father. But while he was still a long way off, his father saw him and felt compassion, and ran and embraced him and kissed him."

LUKE 15:18–20 ESV

Dorothy scribbled in the last letter of her crossword puzzle and sighed. It was her third puzzle of the day. She glanced at the silent phone beside her chair. Her daughter, Samantha, was so very busy with three little girls. One was in dance. And one in soccer. The other was still in diapers and kept her daughter exhausted. But maybe she would call tomorrow. James had a successful law firm. She was happy that her children were thriving. But they didn't seem to have a moment to spare for a chat with their mother anymore. Tomorrow, yes, maybe tomorrow they would call.

Have you been neglecting your heavenly Father? He waits for you to open the line and take a time-out from your schedule to spend quality time with Him. Just like the father of the prodigal son, He's overjoyed when you come. Spend some time with Him in prayer right now.

*Heavenly Father, I'm so sorry when I rush through
my day without talking to You. Renew my thirst
for Your Word. In Jesus' name, amen.*

A New Attitude

*Throw off your old sinful nature and your former way of life,
which is corrupted by lust and deception. Instead, let the Spirit
renew your thoughts and attitudes. Put on your new nature,
created to be like God—truly righteous and holy.*
 EPHESIANS 4:22–24 NLT

Maggie loved her grandmother's four-poster cherry bed. She remembered spending the night as a child, hugged by its cozy mattress. Milk and graham crackers before bed, and whispered secrets with Grandma in the dark. She smiled at the cherished memories. But the finish was cracked and weathered. So she began the painstaking process of stripping off the old finish. She carefully scraped off layer after gunky layer of ruined varnish. It was a messy job. But in the end her grandmother's bed was more beautiful than ever.

Have you begun the hard process of stripping off your old layers of sin? Have your life habits changed since you met Jesus? When we belong to Him, He calls us into a new life. Those old corrupted habits will chain you in darkness. Allow Him to give you a new attitude for your mind—one that seeks His kingdom.

*Jesus, I was burned out and defeated. But through Your strength
I began to change. One false belief, sinful habit, and wrong
attitude at a time, You scraped off the ravages of my former ways
until I began to look more like Your Son. Thank You, Jesus,
that I live in newness and life! In Jesus' name, amen.*

Interrupted

As Jesus was on his way. . .a woman was there who had been subject to bleeding for twelve years. . . . She came up behind him and touched the edge of his cloak, and immediately her bleeding stopped.

LUKE 8:42–44 NIV

The phone rings. Jenny glances at the time. She should have left five minutes ago to run errands and pick Lydia up from school for her doctor's appointment. Then she needs to rush back to pick up Matt after soccer so she can have dinner on the table when Peter gets home. But the caller ID says MOM, and her ailing mother has had a few falls recently. "Hi, Mom. Is everything okay?" she asks as she snaps the baby seat into the van. "Oh honey, I hate to bother you, but I can't get down the basement steps, and I need a few things from the freezer. Could you stop by for a few minutes?"

How do you normally react to unscheduled events that threaten to derail your daily plans? The Bible is filled with stories of Jesus being interrupted. And many of these stories involve miraculous happenings. While He was traveling from place to place, a woman reached out and touched Him. Jesus stopped and healed her.

Don't overlook the unrehearsed, interrupted moments of your life. God is at work in the in-between. When you're interrupted today, pause and look for God's movements.

*Jesus, help me to stop and see
Your work around me. Amen.*

Under His Wings

*"O Jerusalem, Jerusalem, the city that kills the prophets
and stones God's messengers! How often I have wanted
to gather your children together as a hen protects her
chicks beneath her wings, but you wouldn't let me."*

LUKE 13:34 NLT

Tomorrow is your baby daughter's first day of kindergarten. She's your last little one left at home, and your emotions are buckled up to a roller coaster. You gather her school supplies and smile as you place them gently in her new pink My Little Pony backpack. You swipe a stray tear as you make an extra sandwich and pack an extra lunch box this year. You look forward to the joy and excitement of new school memories but mourn the loss of your baby as she grows into a big girl. When she comes bounding into the kitchen to show you her outfit for tomorrow, you pull her into a tight hug. You just can't hold her close enough.

Your heavenly Father feels this same deep love for you. He wants so badly to gather you in because He loves you tenderly. He showers you with outlandish gifts of grace, mercy, belonging, and acceptance. And most of all love. Scoot a little closer to Him today. Feel His gentle arms embrace you.

*Lord, show me when I'm pulling away from You. I don't want to be
separated from Your amazing love. Gather me in, right under Your
protective wings. And hold me near. In Jesus' name, amen.*

A Drop of Mercy

Blessed [content, sheltered by God's promises]
are the merciful, for they will receive mercy.
MATTHEW 5:7 AMP

You hear the angry man berating the waitress for his cold coffee at the table behind you. The poor woman looks ready to snap at him. She snatches his coffee mug from the table and stomps off to the kitchen, while the man complains about the poor service.

The frazzled waitress returns to plop his steaming coffee down in front of him, rattling his silverware as she does. Then she steps over to your table and turns her scowl on you.

What should you do? How would Jesus react in this moment?

You can either smooth her rough day with a smile and kind words, or you can kick her off the cliff of aggravation she's clinging to by responding to her anger with your own.

All it takes is a pinch of mercy and grace to change the course of someone's day. Someone around you is in need of a drop of mercy today. Reflect the beautiful love and mercy of Jesus to them.

God, You are a gracious and merciful God. You have shown me
lavish mercy that I don't deserve. Because I belong to You,
how could I do anything other than scatter Your mercy onto
all those around me. Show me someone today who needs
an extra helping of mercy. In Jesus' name, amen.

Radiant

When Moses came down from Mount Sinai carrying the two Tablets of The Testimony, he didn't know that the skin of his face glowed because he had been speaking with GOD.

EXODUS 34:29 MSG

What must it be like to navigate this dark world without Jesus? If you receive horrifying news of terminal cancer from your physician, if your child is acting out and rebelling, if you lose your job, or even if you just lose your keys, how do you feel without the precious Savior by your side? Hopeless.

But as believers in Jesus we can reflect His light into this dark world that's been overtaken by sin and despair. The more time you spend getting to know God by reading His Word, praying about His desires for your life, praising Him for His goodness, and being still before Him, the more radiant you will become.

What's in your heart will show on your face! Your countenance will glow with the peace and joy of resting in His promises, trusting in His goodness, and basking in His grace. Your friends will see it and want to know the name of your new spa! And you can say, "Forget the spa; rejuvenate in the presence of Jesus!"

Heavenly Father, in Your presence is where I belong. I love being with You both in the quiet and the busyness of my days. I long for the time when I will dwell in the sunshine of Your glory forever. Amen.

Bigger Plans

Now may the God of peace who brought again from the dead our Lord
Jesus, the great shepherd of the sheep, by the blood of the·eternal
covenant, equip you with everything good that you may do his will,
working in us that which is pleasing in his sight, through Jesus Christ.

HEBREWS 13:20–21 ESV

The disciples were hiding in the upper room with the door barred. Fear plagued them. Doubts tormented their minds. What was happening? Their world seemed to be crumbling just when things had been going along so well. But now Jesus was dead. Buried in a borrowed tomb. Had they made a terrible mistake? But what of the miracles? What of the power they had witnessed? It was all so terrifying and confusing.

Then Jesus was there! Alive! Right in their midst. Joy accosted them as they began to grasp the bigger picture of God's plan: A Savior for not only this life but the next. Forgiveness for sins and a new covenant of grace. A kingdom not of this world.[9]

Sometimes we look only at the evil permeating this treacherous place and miss God's movement, His plans, His provision, His hope. Are you locked in an upper room bound in fear? Ask Jesus to join you there and strengthen your faith. Ask Him for the next step in His plans for you.

Jesus, sometimes I miss what You're doing because I'm looking with
earthly eyes. Open my spiritual eyes to Your plans for me. Amen.

---

[9] See John 20:19–23.

Live Generously!

"Whoever wants to be great must become a servant. Whoever wants to be first among you must be your slave. That is what the Son of Man has done: He came to serve, not to be served."

MARK 10:43–45 MSG

We have an invisible person at our house named Not Me. Maybe you have someone by this name living with you too. Not Me is generous with her time and always offers quickly to help with chores and cleanup. Almost every time I ask for assistance, Not Me volunteers.

Sadly, many of us grown-up girls are just as quick to shove Not Me front and center when something needs to be done. But Jesus modeled a different philosophy. He came to serve, not to be a pampered prince.

Really, Lord? But I want to enjoy life too. I don't want to spend my days doing a boring laundry list of chores for other people. Where's the fun in constantly putting someone else ahead of me?

Dial back the whining, sister—oh, sorry, those were my complaints! God's ways are not our ways. And when we use our gifts to bless others, He mysteriously heaps an even greater measure of rewards back on us. And suddenly your service renders you spiritually successful! By giving away, you've multiplied your assets—you're now living in abundant joy, amazing peace, and astounding love. You're stockpiling heavenly riches!

*Lord, show me how to live generously
in service and love. Amen.*

Tenderly Led

"I will win her back once again. I will lead her into the desert and speak tenderly to her there. I will return her vineyards to her and transform the Valley of Trouble into a gateway of hope. She will give herself to me there, as she did long ago when she was young."
HOSEA 2:14–15 NLT

The hiker stumbled and splashed onto her hands and knees in the shallow stream. The floor of this deep hollow was shadowed and chilly. Fear sheeted down her spine as icy as the mountain water she'd landed in. She was lost. And wet. And alone.

Or was she? The sharp crack of a stick pierced the mountain stillness. She jumped up, fearing a nightmarish attack of teeth and claws. But to her immeasurable relief she saw the bright blue vest of her trail guide. She'd been found!

Life may not be cradling you with gentle hands. You may feel battered by hardship and pain. But Jesus longs to speak tender words to your struggling soul. Whether you've been abandoned or abused or suffered from physical or emotional pain, He can transform your trouble into a place of hope. Give yourself to Him. Right in the midst of your hardship, step through His door of hope into freedom. The freedom of acceptance. The liberty of forgiveness. Dear friend, His purpose in your pain could be the redemption of your eternal soul.

Jesus, You don't desire hardship for me, but You can gently redeem it for Your purpose. Amen.

Fortress

How long will you assault me? Would all of you throw me down—this leaning wall, this tottering fence? Surely they intend to topple me from my lofty place; they take delight in lies. With their mouths they bless, but in their hearts they curse. Yes, my soul, find rest in God; my hope comes from him. Truly he is my rock and my salvation; he is my fortress, I will not be shaken.

PSALM 62:3–6 NIV

"Jannie, surely you're not going to eat that chocolate cake, are you? I mean, I'm only looking out for you, sweetie. You have to fit into that bridesmaid dress next month, right?" Your so-called friend's syrupy tone isn't fooling you for a minute. She's always been jealous of your job, your singing voice, your personality. She pretends to be best buds, but her true colors raise every time she attacks your slightly curvier-than-Vogue figure. And she absolutely knows you hate being called Jannie!

Do you ever feel as though you're surrounded by "frenemies"? They say pretty words to your face, but inside they're secretly hoping you tuck your dress into your underwear and parade around the party with your fanny hanging out in the breeze.

Navigating this world is exhausting, but your vulnerable spirit can find a safe place in Jesus. When the enemy assaults you with vicious accusations, looking for weaknesses to exploit, remember that you have a fortress.

Lord, remind me of Your truth in the face of hurtful lies. In Jesus' name, amen.

He Said Yes!

Whatever God has promised gets stamped with the Yes of Jesus. In Him, this is what we preach and pray, the great Amen, God's Yes and our Yes together, gloriously evident. God affirms us, making us a sure thing in Christ, putting his Yes within us. By his Spirit he has stamped us with his eternal pledge—a sure beginning of what he is destined to complete.

2 CORINTHIANS 1:20-22 MSG

"No, you can't have that. No, you can't go there. No, you can't do that." No, no, no, no, no! We hear the disappointing denial of the word *no* all the time, especially if you have young children; your dialogue seems stuck on this dissatisfying response.

But no matter how many promises God has made to you, they are all "Yes!" in Jesus. He has filled you with the Holy Spirit and placed His stamp of ownership on your soul. Yes, you have been made new by the power of His blood. Yes, you can live in abundant joy. Yes, you are His cherished daughter. Yes, you have His supernatural power to resist sin. Yes, everlasting life in the glorious presence of God is yours! Nothing He has spoken to you will go unfulfilled.

Thank You, God, for Your yes. In the name of Jesus, amen!

Faith over Fear

"To whom will you compare me? Or who is my equal?" says the Holy One. Lift up your eyes and look to the heavens: Who created all these? He who brings out the starry host one by one and calls forth each of them by name. Because of his great power and mighty strength, not one of them is missing.

ISAIAH 40:25–26 NIV

Ava lay on a blanket in her yard and took in the breathtaking heavens stretched out above her. The sky was cloaked in velvety darkness and scattered with stars sparkling like gems. The knot of worry in her chest about her mother's health, her husband's upcoming job review, and her son's declining grades in school eased as she realized that God had placed each of those glittering points of light in the universe. If He could call out each star by name, surely He could handle her distressing daily life.

What worries visit your mind at night when the world sleeps? Your life is clutched in the grasp of the Holy One—the living and powerful God of heaven and earth. Yield your life today to the movements of His will. Don't allow the enemy to lie to you. God is not ineffective or insufficient. He is lacking in no way. There is no equal to His greatness!

Father, You are greater than my problems. You are the one who holds everything together. Help me to trust. Amen.

Soul Food

"I am the bread of life. Your fathers ate the manna in the wilderness, and they died. This is the bread that comes down from heaven, so that one may eat of it and not die. I am the living bread that came down from heaven. If anyone eats of this bread, he will live forever. And the bread that I will give for the life of the world is my flesh."

JOHN 6:48–51 ESV

The Thanksgiving spread was impressive. A charming fall centerpiece of pumpkins and squash were nestled in a bed of colorful autumn leaves and acorns. Long-stem, tapered candles glowed softly as wax crept down their lengths. The tantalizing aroma of apples and cinnamon wafted from your favorite pie. Sweet potatoes and corn and spiced carrots all vie for position atop your crisp linen tablecloth. The china sparkles in expectation. And the turkey. To. Die. For.

We indulge our appetites, but in a matter of hours we're feeling hunger pangs and craving something more. Our souls cry out to be filled as well. We partake of the world's buffet—money, perfectly toned abs, accolades, or acceptance—but its only temporary satisfaction. Soon we're empty again.

There is only one spiritual superfood capable of filling your void—the Bread of Life. What would happen if today you abandoned all your to-die-for substitutes for Him—the One who died for you?

Jesus, in You I have found what my soul craves. Amen.

He Knows No Limit

The earth is the LORD's and the fullness thereof, the world and those who dwell therein, for he has founded it upon the seas and established it upon the rivers. Who shall ascend the hill of the LORD? And who shall stand in his holy place?

PSALM 24:1–3 ESV

For the first time Adele stood, toes buried in the soft sand, and gazed out over the vast expanse of the sea. She watched in wonder as the ocean threw its weight and the waves rolled in with mighty force to crash on the beach and unfurl across the sand, wrapping her legs in frothy foam. But each time the sea pulled the rushing water back into itself, into its God-given boundaries. Standing on its edge, she felt small.

We have our boundaries too. These limits that our heavenly Father has set on our lives are for our own good. But our smallness allows us to appreciate His limitlessness. His presence stretches out around us far beyond the ocean's borders. His power exceeds the thundering strength of the most intimidating waves. He created it all. And He is the God of it all. And He is the God of me. And you.

When you reach the limit of your own strength, you will find Him there. At the end of yourself, He waits to unveil to you the immeasurable expanse of His great love, power, and grace.

Lord, in my weakness You are strong. At the end of my strength is Your unfathomable power. Amen.

Come

"Lord, if it's you," Peter replied, "tell me to come to you on the water." "Come," he said. Then Peter got down out of the boat, walked on the water and came toward Jesus.

MATTHEW 14:28–29 NIV

"Pam, grab your helmet and let's go!" But the clearly nervous woman looked skeptically at her borrowed bike. A cycling trip did sound like a wonderful way to experience the fall colors, but she'd just seen a disturbing statistic on the news. "Did you know that over eight hundred people were killed in biking accidents last year? I don't know if this is a good idea."

Are you the adventurous type? Or more likely to hang back, calculating the risk assessment? We tend to be a little hard on the apostle Peter for taking his eyes off Jesus and sinking into the waves. Yet we overlook the fact that Peter is the only one who got out of the boat! And because he did, he walked on the water with Jesus!

Jesus invites you to come too. Come into a deeper relationship with Him. Come and experience the awe of watching God work out His plan. Come and discover the unique purpose He has for your life. Following Jesus onto the waters of faith can lead to miraculous changes in your life. Are you willing to take a risk for Him today? Step out of the boat. See what God will do.

*Lord, give me courage to step into
Your purpose for my life. Amen.*

Remember

"Remember the things I have done in the past. For I alone am God! I am God, and there is none like me. Only I can tell you the future before it even happens. Everything I plan will come to pass."

ISAIAH 46:9–10 NLT

You relax on the back deck of your grandparents' lake house. You've spent part of nearly every summer here. Your grandmother smiles, and the deep creases in her cheeks lift. "I remember when your grandfather took me on our honeymoon trip the year after we were married. We didn't have two pennies to rub together when we got married. So the next year he surprised me with a trip up to this lake. We came here every year after and bought this house when your mama was about ten years old. Your granddad certainly did love this water and seeing his family enjoying it."

Remembering. We cherish our memories of good times and even hard times that strengthened us. It's important not to forget where you've come from because your past has chiseled you into the unique person you are.

God says, "Remember the things I have done in the past." If you find yourself doubting God's goodness, His ability to straighten out the kinks in your day, His love for you, or His power, just look back. You'll see the evidence of His guiding presence and find fresh faith!

Heavenly Father, bring Your past deliverances and mercies to mind when doubt assaults me. Amen.

Misfit

Then the word of the LORD came to him: "This man will not be your heir, but a son who is your own flesh and blood will be your heir." He took him outside and said, "Look up at the sky and count the stars—if indeed you can count them." Then he said to him, "So shall your offspring be." Abram believed the LORD, and he credited it to him as righteousness.

GENESIS 15:4–6 NIV

Have you ever felt inadequate in your faith? This feeling can creep into your thought life, especially after a bout of human stumbling. You tried to keep your footing, read your Bible, pray daily, coach yourself up on your game plan for evading Satan's snares, but you still landed flat-out on your tush in the dirt. I understand. I've had to pick myself up and shake the dirt off too. But don't let your stumble define you. God is in the business of using misfits.

Be encouraged by the imperfect people used greatly by God in scripture.

Abraham lied and didn't exactly trust God to handle things, yet he fathered a nation and was considered righteous.

Moses was a murderer and had a hot temper, yet he led a nation out of slavery and through a sea.

David was an adulterer, a murderer, and not exactly the father of the year, yet he was a man after God's own heart and a great king of Israel.

We've all sinned, but God can still transform you into a woman of virtue. Choose this day to trust in His promises.

Father, I choose to trust You. Amen.

A Place to Belong

*"My Father's house has many rooms; if that were not so, would I
have told you that I am going there to prepare a place for you?
And if I go and prepare a place for you, I will come back and
take you to be with me that you also may be where I am.
You know the way to the place where I am going."*

JOHN 14:2–4 NIV

All humanity shares one inevitable end: we're all going to die one day. Unless of course you're here when Jesus returns—hallelujah! But death isn't the final end to a finite existence. God created us for eternity, and death is just the door. Jesus landed the Satan-crushing, death-defying blow when He gave His life on the cross and rose again three days later.

This world is more like a hallway or merely a front porch to heaven—it sure doesn't seem to provide much protection from foul weather. Friend, there's a better place waiting for us. And God is pulling out all the stops! Imagine a home where the stain of sin is wiped away—perfect immortal bodies, free from pain and illness; people who delight in righteousness, who have no anger, jealousy, or hatred, or steal; a landscape more beautiful than a finely manicured park, with no dead leaves or decayed wood; and the ultimate experience of living in God's glorious presence, day after day after day!

Jesus, thank You for the hope of my forever home. Amen.

Your True Life

*"Therefore I tell you, do not worry about your life, what you will eat
or drink; or about your body, what you will wear. Is not life more than
food, and the body more than clothes? Look at the birds of the air;
they do not sow or reap or store away in barns, and yet your heavenly
Father feeds them. Are you not much more valuable than they?
Can any one of you by worrying add a single hour to your life?"*

MATTHEW 6:25–27 NIV

If you never loosen the tight rein of control and worry you're clutching, you'll never see where God might run with your life. His loving intent is not that your days be strangled with anxiety. We strain for an elusive control over our surroundings that's merely a myth.

Your heavenly Father wants you to grasp His hand in total trust, fully expecting that He is able to provide for your needs, to bring plentiful goodness and abundant joy into your day-to-day journey despite its trials. He wants you to live with an attitude of peace, far from the nasty lies of the enemy. Trust Him with your troubles, and receive victory and freedom to enjoy the colors of a butterfly's wing, to picnic in the sun while your children giggle and dance in the wildflowers, and to lighten someone's burden with a helping hand.

*Father, may I trust You so fully that I can live the
abundant life You intended. In Jesus' name, amen.*

For His Glory

*"The servant given one thousand said, 'Master, I know you have
high standards and hate careless ways, that you demand the best
and make no allowances for error. I was afraid I might disappoint you,
so I found a good hiding place and secured your money. Here it is,
safe and sound down to the last cent.' The master was furious. 'That's a
terrible way to live! It's criminal to live cautiously like that! If you knew
I was after the best, why did you do less than the least? The least you
could have done would have been to invest the sum with the bankers,
where at least I would have gotten a little interest. Take the thousand and
give it to the one who risked the most. And get rid of this "play-it-safe"
who won't go out on a limb. Throw him out into utter darkness.' "*

MATTHEW 25:24–30 MSG

What thing in your life makes your heart skip in anticipation? Have you
ever considered that God planted that desire, that special talent, in your
makeup for His glory? Your actions here on earth do matter. God is whisper-
ing to you today, *"That thing you love to do—I gave it to you for a reason—
come and do it for Me!"*

*God, I give You my talents.
Use them for Your purpose. Amen.*

Walk by Faith

So we are always of good courage. We know that while we are at home in the body we are away from the Lord, for we walk by faith, not by sight. Yes, we are of good courage, and we would rather be away from the body and at home with the Lord. So whether we are at home or away, we make it our aim to please him.

2 CORINTHIANS 5:6–9 ESV

The world says that faith is blind. But it's really our eyes that can deceive us by what they *don't* see. Our faith recognizes that this world isn't all there is to life. It's our trust in what we hope for—the things we know are waiting for us in eternity but can't yet see from our earthly vantage point—that keeps us going and gives our faith something to grab on to in the hard times.

But how do we know a fabulous eternal life awaits? The eyes of your faith can see the truth, and your long, intimate journey with God provides the evidence. Make it your goal to please Him, to take long walks with Him, to look for His movement around you, and to find out all you can about the Creator who loves you, and then your absolute certainty of the truth of all His promises will deepen.

God, open my eyes of faith. I want to step out confidently, knowing every word You've spoken is concrete truth. Amen.

Show Your Love

The third time he said to him, "Simon son of John, do you love me?" Peter was hurt because Jesus asked him the third time, "Do you love me?" He said, "Lord, you know all things; you know that I love you." Jesus said, "Feed my sheep."

JOHN 21:17 NIV

Our hearts swell with love for our kids. When they're babies, we rock them and cuddle them and stay up all night comforting them through stuffy noses and teething. And we don't mind enduring sleeplessness because of our love. We show them how much we care over and over again. And we long for the day we'll hear the words *I love you* returned back to us.

God loves all of His children with a depth of affection unfathomable to our limited minds. And He doesn't just say the words, He proves them in action. God loves you so much that He sent His beloved Son to die for you to heal the rift between you.

Following Jesus isn't an empty religion of rituals; it's a deep, abiding relationship with the God who loves you. Jesus told Peter if he loved Him to feed His sheep. He longs for you to return His love as well. But He wants more than empty words.

Show Him your love today through your actions.

Father, Your love is total and full, beautiful and amazing. I love You too. Amen.

A Bit of Kindness

Put on then, as God's chosen ones, holy and beloved, compassionate hearts, kindness, humility, meekness, and patience, bearing with one another and, if one has a complaint against another, forgiving each other; as the Lord has forgiven you, so you also must forgive.

COLOSSIANS 3:12–13 ESV

The little girl splashes through puddles in her pink polka-dot rubber boots. She picks up a small stone and throws it into the pond where her dad is fishing. She stares in amazement at the widening circle of ripples stretching across the surface of the water. "Look, Daddy! It's getting bigger and bigger."

Kindness operates a lot like that. It might seem like a small thing to you, holding a door for a loaded-down mom, raking your elderly neighbor's leaves, smiling at that grumpy coworker, but kindness expands just like the ripples on a pond. Each kind act touches the life of someone beside you and brings hope and a spark of brightness to their spirit. It might even set off a chain reaction of kindness to the next person she meets!

God's kindness to us is also attractive. His grace draws us in to hear His truth. Your kindness can also draw others to Jesus. In a world fueled by self-focus and me-me-me attitudes, anyone who sees your kindness will wonder why you'd bother. You never know what far-reaching results a little drop of kindness might have.

*God, show me where a bit of kindness could
spread Your love around me. Amen.*

Never Beyond His Reach

God raised us up with Christ and seated us with him in the heavenly realms in Christ Jesus, in order that in the coming ages he might show the incomparable riches of his grace, expressed in his kindness to us in Christ Jesus. For it is by grace you have been saved, through faith—and this is not from yourselves, it is the gift of God—not by works, so that no one can boast.

 EPHESIANS 2:6–9 NIV

Beloved, do you have secrets? Dark closets in your soul that you are hesitant to open because you fear the ghosts of your past who inhabit them? Maybe you've said terrible words, maybe you've done horrible things, or maybe you've felt shameful emotions. Or perhaps you've been the victim of another's vicious words or deeds. Whatever the case, there's hope.

You can never outrun God's mercy or cross the borders of His grace. No matter what you've done or what's been done to you, you're never beyond His reach. No matter how dirty the enemy makes you feel, God can lift your face and wash away your stains in the crimson flood of Jesus' blood. He can clothe you in mercy and seat you with Jesus at His table in heaven. Bring your secrets to the light of His forgiveness, and bask in the glow of His extravagant grace.

Jesus, my shame is gone! My fear is gone! I never imagined I could feel clean again. But You washed it all away. Thank You. Amen.

You Can Find Him

Starting from scratch, he made the entire human race and made the earth hospitable, with plenty of time and space for living so we could seek after God, and not just grope around in the dark but actually find him. He doesn't play hide-and-seek with us. He's not remote; he's near. We live and move in him, can't get away from him!

ACTS 17:26–28 MSG

"Ready or not, here I come!" You loved hide-and-seek as a child. You were the best seeker. But you remember a time when you looked and looked and couldn't find your sister anywhere. You were so frustrated you wanted to shout. Then you heard a little snicker. She'd stacked some boxes in the garage so that a hollow spot was left in the middle and then crawled in and placed the last box in the hole. The perfect hiding spot, much to your exasperation.

At times we look around for God and can't seem to see Him, but God isn't playing games with you. He wants to be found and known and loved by you. He wants a deep and meaningful relationship with you, His beloved daughter. God doesn't delight in confusion and tricks, and He won't hold Himself back from you if you search for Him. He's near. Ask God to step into the light. And He will show Himself to you.

God, thank You for being closer to me than I imagined. Walk with me today. Amen.

You Are Accepted

"Those the Father has given me will come to me, and I will never reject them. For I have come down from heaven to do the will of God who sent me, not to do my own will. And this is the will of God, that I should not lose even one of all those he has given me, but that I should raise them up at the last day."

JOHN 6:37–39 NLT

Who among us has lived the ten-minute frenzy otherwise known as "Oh no, someone is coming over—quick, throw all this stuff in the closet, put everything in the dishwasher, and clean that toilet!" Raise your hand, sister. There's no judgment here. And if that's not you, kudos to your mad organizational skills.

Isn't it a relief that we don't have to clean ourselves up for God? He's already familiar with all our ugly messes anyway. We're free to bring every problem to Him. Don't listen to Satan's lies. You haven't done anything He hasn't seen before. You can't shock Him with your sin. Instead He says, "Come"—without fear of rejection, without punishment and shame. There's a place for you at God's banquet. Pull up a chair and take your place. Daughter of the King, His grace covers all.

Lord, I haven't been honest with You.
I've tried to hide my problems. But I'm
coming to You now. Forgive me. Amen.

Fingerprints of the Creator

*For ever since the world was created, people have seen
the earth and sky. Through everything God made, they can
clearly see his invisible qualities—his eternal power and
divine nature. So they have no excuse for not knowing God.*

ROMANS 1:20 NLT

TV crime drama is addictive because we humans like evidence. We can't wait to see what the detectives uncover and find out "whodunit" by following a trail of clues.

God has not left us without evidence of Himself either. In fact, He planted us firmly in a world teeming with proof of His existence. It stretches above you in a clear night sky sprinkled with sparkling stars. It's in the burning light of dawn that unfurls from the horizon. It's in the dew drops that cling to spring tulips and the crickets' song that follows a sweltering summer afternoon. You can find it in the blazing fall colors and the stark winter snow.

Only a divine God of eternal power could paint a world with the proof of His care. He exists. He's here with you. He cares! We have no excuse for not knowing Him. Open your eyes and see the signs. Walk through His creation today. Search for His fingerprints of love, and you will find Him there.

*Father, open my eyes to all
Your invisible qualities. Amen.*

Perfect Peace

Peace I leave with you; my peace I give to you.
Not as the world gives do I give to you. Let not
your hearts be troubled, neither let them be afraid.
JOHN 14:27 ESV

You look down at your phone screen—blank. Your battery is dead again. *What is it with cell phones?* you wonder. *Why do their batteries seem to choke on a calculated last gasp just after your contract has expired?*

In this world, things that seem too good to be true often are. No matter how generous someone's motives seem, most of the time there's a self-serving angle. Is anyone here completely selfless and good? Only God! This world's hidden strings aren't attached to His gifts. The peace He offers is legitimate and guaranteed for all eternity. It won't wheeze its dying breath two hours after the warranty expires. His unlimited coverage permeates every facet of your life.

Is worry leaving you exhausted? His peace covers that. Are busy schedules leaving you frantic? His peace covers that too. Is fear over the future robbing your joy? Yep, His peace has you covered.

His gifts are not an illusion. You can actually live enveloped in His peace when you hold firmly to His grasp and surrender to His will. Trust Him today. You won't need a money-back guarantee.

Jesus, thank You that You don't offer false promises.
I can trust You to keep me in perfect peace. Amen.

You Are Redeemed

In their fright the women bowed down with their faces to the ground, but the men said to them, "Why do you look for the living among the dead? He is not here; he has risen! Remember how he told you, while he was still with you in Galilee."

LUKE 24:5–6 NIV

Our heavenly Father delights in redeeming the fallen things of this world. Our failures can become His landslide victories and our weaknesses His strength. That Easter morning so long ago, Jesus delivered a devil-defeating, hell-busting blow to the enemy. He redeemed death into life. Jesus broke the chains of our captivity to sin and death—so we need no longer fear death's finality.

"Why do you look for the living among the dead?" the angel asked. The women were confused. They hadn't yet realized that the empty tomb symbolized the fullness of new life. And the dawning realization that Jesus was alive brought a flood of hope. Their despair changed to dancing. Light flooded into the darkness of this world. Their lives would never be the same again. An empty tomb proved Jesus could not be held by death's constraints. He lives!

Jesus changes lives yet today, and He can change yours too.

Lord, thank You for a redeemed life in You. Amen.

Aged to Perfection

*"Stand up in the presence of the aged, show respect
for the elderly and revere your God. I am the LORD."*
LEVITICUS 19:32 NIV

The old dusty bottle was nestled in a cocoon of cobwebs in the back corner of your mom's basement shelf. The label was too faded to read, so you grabbed it and started to chuck it into the garbage bag when your mother touched your arm. "Oh, don't toss that out with the trash, honey. That's a bottle of wine from my wedding to your dad. It was a fine wine then. I'm sure it's even better now that it's aged a bit more. That bottle is worth quite a bit."

Sometimes our attitude toward the elderly is just as misguided. Their exterior has lost the sparkle of newness and looks a bit worse for wear, so we assume they've lost their value. Some even think they've outlived their usefulness.

But God values the life of each and every person. Each one is precious to Him, created in His image with a specific purpose in mind. And you can't outlive God's purpose for your life. But our definition of useful and God's definition might not match up. Sit with them and soak in their wisdom. Hold their hand and listen. After all, their purpose could be to share with you the insight they've accumulated after decades of walking with Jesus.

*God, help me see the value of each person
through Your eyes. In Jesus' name, amen.*

In Charge

Our God is in the heavens;
he does all that he pleases.
PSALM 115:3 ESV

The little girl was thrilled to be at the county fair. She had waited all year to eat sweet fluffy clouds of cotton candy and experience the carnival rides again. She loved the race cars and ran to her favorite pink car. After she was buckled in, the ride jerked into motion. She grasped the steering wheel in her small hands and smoothly spun it around, guiding her car into the turns and up and down. She felt grown up and powerful!

But in reality she had only the illusion of control, as her steering wheel couldn't affect the car's direction at all. As grown-ups we still suffer from delusions of grandeur when it comes to our perceived control over our world. Sometimes a taste of power has us convinced we can plan our destiny without God. Other times we seem to be convinced that our worrying and anxiety will somehow prevent unwanted things from entering our universe.

Thankfully we belong to a God who is large and in charge. His plans will come to pass as He pleases. But we can rest in the knowledge that all our mistakes and power plays will never succeed in wrestling control from His grasp. So relax today in the knowledge that He loves you and that you belong to the powerful God of creation. He's got this!

Lord, I surrender to Your control. I belong
to You, who has the power. Amen.

A Cleaner Purpose

Run from anything that stimulates youthful lusts. Instead,
pursue righteous living, faithfulness, love, and peace. Enjoy the
companionship of those who call on the Lord with pure hearts.

2 TIMOTHY 2:22 NLT

A decadent chocolate cake topped with mounds of creamy dark frosting—your fingers lift a fork almost before your brain registers the sweet smell of sugar. So. Very. Delicious. Donuts, pies, brownies, and don't even mention those ladyfingers from the bakery. You crave those sugary creations.

But then your doctor says you're at risk for diabetes. So you pledge to clean up your diet and eliminate your favorite ingredient—sugar. At first you couldn't get donuts out of your head. The smell of your friend's candy bar almost sent you into a relapse. But gradually, as you practiced healthy eating, it got easier. Your tastes began to change. And now you actually *crave* vegetables. Yes, you can walk away from that French éclair without a backward glance!

When we first come to Jesus, it can be difficult to give up the ways of this world. But as you begin to live on a diet of the Bread of Life, your tastes for the things of this world will sour. Keep turning to His Word when the hankering for old ways hits you, and soon you'll be craving the pure living habits of faithfulness, love, and obedience.

Father, give me strength to resist temptation.
You have a better purpose for me. Amen.

Your True Purpose

*Do your best. Work from the heart for your real Master, for God,
confident that you'll get paid in full when you come into your inheritance.
Keep in mind always that the ultimate Master you're serving is Christ.*
COLOSSIANS 3:23–24 MSG

A tower of dirty dishes glares at you over the rim of your sink. And another leaning pile teeters on the countertop. Sighing, you pick up a bowl and glance inside. Yesterday's mashed potatoes are caked on like dried cement. This is going to require some serious scouring. And no one is going to do it for you.

You have a choice to make. And it involves your attitude. Ouch! No one enjoys an attitude check. *Isn't it enough, Lord, that we just get through our daily tasks? You mean I actually have to bring You glory out of this pile of pans? Okay fine—one attitude adjustment coming up.*

As you plunk the first dish into the water, you thank God for taking your dirty, sin-stained life and washing away all the grime, for shining you up and showing you His purpose for your days. Your daughter wanders into the kitchen, and you chat with her about how Jesus cleans up our hearts, just like you are scrubbing pots. The next thing you know you're singing praises to God in your sparkling kitchen!

*God, my true purpose is to work for You
in whatever task is before me. Amen.*

Corral Your Thoughts

The weapons of our warfare are not of the flesh but have divine power to destroy strongholds. We destroy arguments and every lofty opinion raised against the knowledge of God, and take every thought captive to obey Christ.

2 CORINTHIANS 10:4–5 ESV

"Get back here, Coco!" Elaine slammed the garage door to prevent her cat's escape. She needed to get her to the vet by nine. And now she was going to be late. She lunged for the frisky feline, only to send it scampering across the workbench—overturning a flowerpot and trailing dirty footprints behind. A *meow* sounded from the shelf, and Elaine grabbed at the flash of black fur. A jar of peaches crashed to the floor. Great! Now her pants were splattered with sticky juice. Coco slunk out from the shadows and lapped up the peaches. Shaking her head, Elaine grabbed the little menace and deposited her inside her crate.

Our thoughts can also wreak havoc on our lives when we allow them to run loose. One concern enters our head and, if left unattended, can spill a whole can of worry worms. Before you can say, "Scat, cat!" you're wringing your hands and headed for the Tylenol bottle.

But God doesn't intend for you to be ruled by random thoughts. Even though it can seem as hopeless as herding cats, corner those thoughts! Speak God's truth and demolish the devil's lies.

Heavenly Father, show me when my thoughts are running wild and leading me into sin. Amen.

Your Kingdom Purpose

*He has told you, O man, what is good; and what
does the LORD require of you but to do justice, and
to love kindness, and to walk humbly with your God?*

MICAH 6:8 ESV

Olivia ran through her mental to-do list: *throw in the laundry, take that steak out of the freezer, load the dishwasher. . .* She lost her train of thought when her youngest daughter skipped into the kitchen, grinning and waving her latest coloring masterpiece. "Mama, look what I did! I stayed in the lines so good!" Olivia glanced at her daughter's paper while mentally straining to remember the rest of her list. She knew she was forgetting something. "That's nice, sweetie." Her daughter's smile faltered a little.

Oh, that's it! She needed paper plates for the cookout. And ketchup, maybe? She opened the refrigerator to check on the status of their condiments. "Mom!" her oldest daughter called from upstairs. "Can you come here? I need to ask you something." Olivia sighed and glanced around for her cookbook. "Not now, honey. I'm busy."

Sound familiar? Too often we're fatally nearsighted and hyperfocused on finishing whatever task has captured our attention, and we miss the greater purpose God has given us. What kingdom work have you overlooked because you're distracted? Are you loving the ones in your care? Are you spreading kindness and teaching your children how to walk with Jesus? Or are you distracted by eternally inconsequential details?

Lord, may I not overlook my kingdom work today. Amen.

Straight on to Heaven

*And such were some of you. But you were washed,
you were sanctified, you were justified in the name
of the Lord Jesus Christ and by the Spirit of our God.*

1 CORINTHIANS 6:11 ESV

Apprehension tenses your shoulders. Your fears are confirmed by your helpful son in the backseat. "Mom, we've already been down this street before. We're back where we started!" Hmm, maybe shutting off your GPS wasn't such a great idea. But you were sure you knew where you were going.

Have you ever gotten overconfident, taken your eyes off Jesus for a moment, and found yourself back in the same place where you started? Peter experienced a little of that as he looked away from Jesus during his stroll on the sea. He sank. And you will too. Thankfully Jesus was there to pull him out.

This world can be pretty persuasive: "No one will notice if you skip a Sunday now and then to sleep in or catch up on grocery shopping." "It's okay if you pass on that bit of news you heard about your friend." "Your coworker deserved every last word you said to her—and probably more."

Be careful, dear one. Without the guiding truth of scripture, you could end up circling right back to sins that held you captive in the past.

*Heavenly Father, the words "such were some of you" are so sweet.
Were. In the past. Guide me straight on till heaven. Amen.*

Courage to Be Real

So speak encouraging words to one another. Build up hope so you'll all be together in this, no one left out, no one left behind.

1 THESSALONIANS 5:11 MSG

Social media is great for staying connected, but it's also far too easy to edit your life right out of reality and into your perfect version of yourself. Have you ever cropped out the mess along the edge of your picture? Be honest! Sure you have—when in reality a disaster lies just beyond the border.

In our Christian life it's oh so tempting to do exactly the same thing. You might scream at your kids in the car and paint on a hallelujah smile as soon as your feet cross the sanctified threshold of the church doors. Or perhaps you've neglected your Bible, but you dust it off and place it back on the coffee table because your church friends are coming over for dinner. What? You've never done that?

Sweet, struggling sister, Jesus never called anyone to be perfect—He called you to persevere in spite of your missteps. Ain't nobody perfect—only Jesus! We've all sinned and fallen short of the glory of God—that's hardly a shocker to anyone with a Bible. And if you pretend to have it all together, you may miss God's purpose for your trials. When you come through tough waters, you can turn around and help those struggling behind you.

Lord, give me courage to be real in my faith. Amen.

Reach New Heights

He gives power to the faint, and to him who has no might
he increases strength. Even youths shall faint and be weary,
and young men shall fall exhausted; but they who wait for the
LORD shall renew their strength; they shall mount up with wings like
eagles; they shall run and not be weary; they shall walk and not faint.
ISAIAH 40:29–31 ESV

The eagle catches an updraft and soars to new heights. It hangs suspended in the air with seemingly effortless abandon. Its body is held perfectly still, almost as if completely at rest, as it is carried higher and higher by the arms of the wind.

Do you greet the new day feeling renewed? Or are you left tired and ragged from the relentless demands of your daily schedule? Life today happens at high speed, and patience seems to have been scrapped from our makeup in favor of a more streamlined design. We want our food fast, our communication instant, and that new doodad we ordered delivered yesterday.

It isn't God's plan for you to merely trudge through the day. If you're worn thin, examine your activities and your priorities. Ask God for His input on your to-do list. Pause. Wait. Breathe in. Breathe out. Pray and be still. Seek God's movement. Ride the updraft of His will instead of striving all on your own. And be refreshed, even as you soar.

Father, teach me patience and trust
so I can rest in Your will. Amen.

Try Jesus

God, you did everything you promised, and I'm thanking you with all my heart. You pulled me from the brink of death, my feet from the cliff-edge of doom. Now I stroll at leisure with God in the sunlit fields of life.

"Judy, your complexion looks amazing. Why, you look ten years younger! What skin treatment do you use?" Judy smiled broadly. "I'm so excited. I tried this essential-oil blend on my face. Just a couple drops in my moisturizer morning and night, and my lines are fading away and my skin is so bright. You have to try it!"

Isn't it exciting to share new solutions with others? Whether it's a "miracle" beauty cream or a delicious recipe, we love telling one another about our discoveries. But why is it when Jesus is the solution to a problem we see that we're much more hesitant to speak up? Why not share how His peace has soothed your anxiety or how His joy has cured your depression? Or how your anger has cooled in the refreshing pool of His grace?

Next time you see someone struggling, share with them the transforming power of walking through this life with Jesus as your constant companion. After all, you should be excited! He smooths out the wrinkles in your character and eases the frown lines from your face with His joy and peace.

Lord, may I be bold in sharing what You've done for me. Amen.

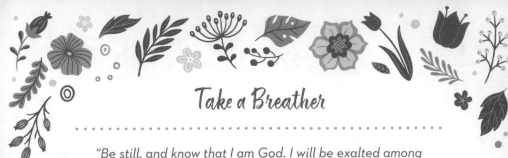

Take a Breather

"Be still, and know that I am God. I will be exalted among the nations, I will be exalted in the earth!" The LORD of hosts is with us; the God of Jacob is our fortress.

PSALM 46:10–11 ESV

Busy. Busy. Busy. So many activities occupy our time and our focus. And it's tempting to share all those in-medias-res snapshots on social media. Busyness is the new status symbol of the day. When others want to spend time with us, replying with "Let me see when I can pencil you in" or "I'll just check my schedule" makes our lives sound so much weightier than a simple "Yes, I'm free."

And someone of even greater importance wants a slot in your schedule as well. God wants you to take a time-out in all your self-important scampering about and then listen. He often speaks in a whisper. So it's in the still hush of the pause that you will hear His voice. Our minds are usually rushing just as fast as our feet—scrolling through to-do lists and worries at landscape-blurring speeds, so even if we do still our bodies for a bit, our minds are far from rest.

Find a quiet, solitary place. Be still. Shush those rampant, anxiety-inducing thoughts. Listen. Meditate on scripture. Know that He is God—omniscient, powerful, unchanging. The realization will bring you peace and security, and maybe even a gentle reality check about your self-importance.

God, keep me humble. Speak into my stillness. Amen.

Pray First

If you don't know what you're doing, pray to the Father. He loves to help. You'll get his help, and won't be condescended to when you ask for it. Ask boldly, believingly, without a second thought.
JAMES 1:5–6 MSG

"Mom, I think I messed up." Your daughter hands you her latest sewing craft, the thread snarled in a tangle. "I thought I knew how to do this stitch, but I don't. Can you show me how?"

As adults, we too often make this same error. "Oops, Lord, I ran ahead and made a mess—again. I should have prayed first!" We forget to ask God for help when we need it. Do we think God is uninterested in our problems, or do we assume He won't answer us?

Friend, you don't need to wring your hands in worry when indecision plagues you. Pray! Are you struggling with a decision about your future? Ask Him. Do you need help learning how to connect with your kids? Ask Him. Are you in a strained relationship and can't figure out how to restore it? Ask Him.

Your Father in heaven gives His guidance generously and without condescension. He doesn't want you wandering around blind! Pray and search scripture for His wisdom. His Word is living and applicable to every part of your life. He wants you to have the answers you need to live within the bounds of His purpose for you. Just ask!

*Father, may I come to You first for help,
before I make mistakes. Amen.*

More Like Him

If someone claims, "I know him well!" but doesn't keep his commandments, he's obviously a liar. His life doesn't match his words. But the one who keeps God's word is the person in whom we see God's mature love. This is the only way to be sure we're in God. Anyone who claims to be intimate with God ought to live the same kind of life Jesus lived.

1 JOHN 2:4–6 MSG

"Look, Mom!" Your seven-year-old waves you into the bathroom and points proudly at the now-sparkling porcelain throne—the one surrounded by wadded-up paper towels and blue-tinged puddles. "I cleaned. Just like you!" You catch that scolding tone before it leaves your mouth and smile. Because puddles and all, she tried to be just like you.

Who are you becoming? We belong to a holy God who asks us to be holy as He is holy. We were bought from sin by Jesus' precious blood and asked to walk like Jesus walked. Are you growing to be more and more like Him, to reflect the nature of the God you belong to?

You aren't going to be perfect. You're going to take a few missteps. You might even end up splashing the floor with toilet water. But the more time you spend in the company of Jesus, the more your life will look like His. His gentle kindness, loving forgiveness, total joy, and unshakable peace will take up residence in your character.

Lord, teach me to follow in Your footsteps. Amen.

He's Delighted with You

The King of Israel, the LORD, is in your midst; you shall never again
fear evil. On that day it shall be said to Jerusalem: "Fear not, O Zion;
let not your hands grow weak. The LORD your God is in your midst,
a mighty one who will save; he will rejoice over you with gladness;
he will quiet you by his love; he will exult over you with loud singing."
ZEPHANIAH 3:15–17 ESV

Does anyone like me? Who hasn't heard this insecure thought echo in their mind? Our world is saturated with instant communication, yet depression and suicide rates are rising, and many people feel disconnected and invisible. Even if we seem surrounded by friends, we often feel disliked and unaccepted.

The enemy will take this opportunity to whisper something evil. He'll tell you that you're overlooked and unappreciated by everyone. But God's Word says something different, something hopeful and encouraging—something bright! Even if everyone else on earth were apathetic to your presence, your heavenly Father takes great delight in you. He loves you and rejoices over you. He's so ecstatic when you enter into His presence that He sings with joy when you arrive. He sculpted every cell of your being and shaped every plane of your personality, and He thinks you're absolutely delightful!

God, You're pleased to see me!
Thank You so much for Your tender care. Amen.

Gloriously New

But there's far more to life for us. We're citizens of high heaven!
We're waiting the arrival of the Savior, the Master, Jesus Christ,
who will transform our earthy bodies into glorious bodies like his own. He'll
make us beautiful and whole with the same powerful skill by
which he is putting everything as it should be, under and around him.
PHILIPPIANS 3:21 MSG

After my grandmother died of breast cancer, my mom had a dream. In it she saw her mother glowing with happiness, youth, and health. She was whole again and more beautiful than ever. She knew that God was comforting her and saying, "It's okay. She's no longer in pain, and she's better than she ever was before. She's perfectly wonderful in My presence."

Oh, what a day when we will receive our resurrection bodies! The Bible says that we'll be raised imperishable, glorious, and powerful (see 1 Corinthians 15:42–44). After His resurrection Jesus did amazing things like appear and disappear, yet He could also eat and drink.

The Bible offers a glimpse Jesus' return: "In a moment, in the twinkling of an eye, at the last trumpet. . .we shall be changed. For this perishable body must put on the imperishable, and this mortal body must put on immortality" (1 Corinthians 15:52–53 ESV).

Whatever we look like, the pain of this world will no longer plague us, and we'll be gloriously happy in His presence—forever!

God, I will be steadfast in my work for You
here because glory awaits! Amen.

Attitude of Thanksgiving

Be persistent and devoted to prayer, being alert and focused in your prayer life with an attitude of thanksgiving.
COLOSSIANS 4:2 AMP

Elaine muttered to herself and grabbed a cleaning rag. Her husband had left his beard clippings all over the sink—again. And her kids' cast-off clothes lay forgotten on the floor. Some days she felt like the maid. She swiped the sink clean just as her phone chimed with a text. It was her prayer chain: PLEASE PRAY FOR CHRISTIE. HER HUSBAND JUST DIED OF A HEART ATTACK.

Elaine gasped softly. Christie's husband was just a few years older than her own. Gone. She immediately sat down on the side of the tub to pray. Conviction about her poor attitude squeezed her chest. "God, I'm so sorry. Forgive my ungrateful heart. Comfort Christie and support her with Your love. Thank You, Father, for my husband. Thank You that I'm not alone and that I have someone to clean up after. He works so hard, and he's such a good father. And thank You for my kids. They are my joys. God, thank You for an amazing life full of blessings and another brand-new day to love each other."

Friend, don't get stuck in a mud bog of complaining. An attitude of thanksgiving changes your perspective. It allows you to name your blessings, look them in the face, and recognize God's extravagant goodness. When you're tempted to grumble, thank God for His blessings instead!

Father, thank You for blessing me! Amen.

Precious Thoughts

How precious to me are your thoughts, O God!
PSALM 139:17 ESV

Our thoughts can really take us for a ride. Our emotions sometimes seem set on a roller-coaster course—carrying us ecstatically high before we're screaming down into a pit. But we don't have to dwell on every stray thought that pops into our minds. Our emotions may be drawn to the drama of that roller coaster, but we don't have to get on it with them.

We can control what we think. And we should! The enemy would set your focus on thoughts that will lead you away from God—fear, anxiety, bitterness, anger. Satan would hitch your thoughts to that car and drag you up and down the track until your spirit is black and blue. But you can *choose* to get off. That's right. It's your choice what you will think about and who you will become: "For as he thinks in his heart, so is he" (Proverbs 23:7 AMP).

It's vital that you manage your mind and nurture it with wholesome, life-giving thoughts from God's Word instead of feeding it a steady diet of the enemy's lies. Try buckling your mind to God's way of thinking today: "Whatever is true, whatever is honorable, whatever is just, whatever is pure, whatever is lovely, whatever is commendable, if there is any excellence, if there is anything worthy of praise, think about these things" (Philippians 4:8 ESV).

*God, I choose excellent, rejuvenating thoughts today
that will lead me into Your purpose for me. Amen.*

Forward into Freedom

"Why is the LORD bringing us into this land, to fall by the sword?...
Would it not be better for us to go back to Egypt?"
NUMBERS 14:3 ESV

Moses led the Israelites into freedom after four hundred years of slavery, but once they entered the wilderness all they could think about was how good it had been in Egypt. Their present difficulty had them looking back through rose-colored glasses at their previous slavery.

And how like us. Our fickle minds edit out the nasty parts of our former bondage to harsh masters like shame, fear, and addiction, and hoodwink us into craving the chains we just escaped. There's comfort in the familiar. Walking away from the past and into the barren wilderness with God can be difficult and daunting. When we're feeling the pinch of our rehabilitation in the desert of God's rehab center, it's easy to crave old, comfortable things—even ones that are bad for us.

Be encouraged, dear one. Casting off old thought patterns and habits is hard. But God isn't leading you into the wilderness to stay. His plans for your life lead through the barren grounds, which reveal who God is and strengthen your faith, into the promised land of an abundant new life of freedom with God.

Father, help me to remember that Your plans
of freedom for me are in front, not behind.
They lie on the other side of the wilderness. Amen.

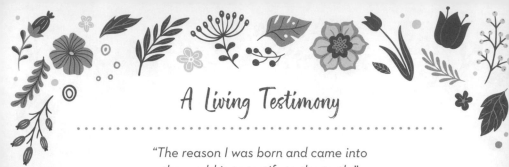

A Living Testimony

*"The reason I was born and came into
the world is to testify to the truth."*

JOHN 18:37 NIV

Truth shines in today's society of fake news, perfect social-media pages, insincere politicians, and photoshopped advertisements. Surrounded by false fronts, we are tempted to don masks of our own and join the pretenders. But if we're willing to live out our walk with Jesus, honestly and openly, in front of our family, friends, and neighbors, the truth of God's message will be proved by our joy in spite of our hardships, our peace in the midst of turmoil, and our selfless love in a selfish world.

Jesus came to testify to the truth. Another definition of *testify* is "to give evidence." Jesus came to give us evidence of God's great plan for mankind: our sin, God's love, forgiveness through Jesus' death and resurrection, the Holy Spirit transforming our lives from within, and the hope of an eternal future with Him. Jesus is the evidence!

Your authentic life for God can make a difference too. As a follower of Jesus, you're called to testify about the changing power of God in your life. Live a real faith—one where you're honest about your struggles and about how God breaks through your problems. The world will notice that you're different. And your light will draw people to Jesus.

Lord, make my life a living testimony to Your truth. Amen.

The Peace of Belonging

"I have said these things to you, that in me you may have peace. In the world you will have tribulation. But take heart; I have overcome the world."

JOHN 16:33 ESV

This world is made up of one trying experience after another. We're plagued with distress and suffering. And that's exactly how Jesus said it would be: "In the world you will have tribulation." If we were to stop there, His words would be downright discouraging. But take heart, just like He said, because there's more.

Jesus didn't leave us tormented in this place of turmoil with no escape hatch. Yes, He did say that living in this world would be hard. Sin reigns here, and we bleed under its iron fist of suffering. Death and disease, heartache and pain, fear and darkness—sometimes the ache of just being here feels like too much to bear. But then Jesus gave us hope: "I have said these things to you, that in me you may have peace. . . . Take heart; I have overcome the world." *In Him.* Jesus is the only One who can bring tranquility to your soul—in Him your future is secure.

If you believe Jesus, He can calm whatever harrowing storm you're facing. When fear grips you, ask yourself if you truly think that your problem is bigger than God. Take heart. There's peace beyond understanding when you belong to Him.

Lord, my troubles may be great, but You are greater. Amen.

The Sweet Perfume of Jesus

*But thank God! He has made us his captives and continues to
lead us along in Christ's triumphal procession. Now he uses us
to spread the knowledge of Christ everywhere, like a sweet
perfume. Our lives are a Christ-like fragrance rising up to God. . . .
To those who are being saved, we are a life-giving perfume.*

2 CORINTHIANS 2:14–16 NLT

Spring smells so fresh! After shivering for months under winter's harsh breath, you step outside into the welcoming sunshine and inhale deeply the scent of new life. The fragrance of lilacs and fresh-cut grass perfumes the breeze. It smells so heavenly you can't resist cutting a few blooms for your table so you can breathe in their sweet fragrance a little while longer.

Does your life smell as sweet to God? Does the fresh scent of hope and belonging waft from your everyday actions? As believers in Jesus, we are meant to be a life-giving perfume that saturates the air around us with an irresistible aroma of hope and new life. This world is filled to the brim with repulsive, stinky attitudes. People will notice if you step into the room with the lingering scent of your Savior clinging to your thoughts and actions. They'll want to know the name of the fragrance you're wearing. And you can say *Jesus!*

*Father, may my actions today attract
people to Your life-giving Son. Amen.*

Together Forever

He will swallow up death forever. The Lord God will wipe away all tears and take away forever all insults and mockery against his land and people. The Lord has spoken—he will surely do it!

ISAIAH 25:8 TLB

Agatha sank into the couch cushions and stared at the worn leather recliner entrenched on the opposite side of the dim room—the *empty* leather recliner. Loneliness assaulted her. She was a widow now. Never again would her beloved husband of forty-five years shake out the morning paper and peruse the headlines over coffee in his favorite chair. Never again in this life could she ask his advice or share amusement with him over things only he would understand. She would walk out her remaining days bearing the heavy burden of his absence.

Heaven is going to be a fantastically wonderful place. Imagine the undiluted joy of being with your loved ones and knowing it will never end, of being in the unfiltered presence of our God. Here on earth our love and joy are tainted by the fear of loss and death; we fear the sharp prick of separation. Our greatest sorrow began ages past in a garden when we were separated from the Creator who loved us first and best. But God in His unimaginable mercy has promised to remove this pall of separation and restore the joy of our fellowship forever!

Father, You have given me the hope of an eternal future without fear. Amen.

His Compassion

" 'He will wipe every tear from their eyes. There will be no more death' or mourning or crying or pain, for the old order of things has passed away."
REVELATION 21:4 NIV

Sometimes horrible things happen. Our pain and grief cut sharply into the tender fabric of our hearts. People express their sympathy, but then they turn back to their lives, and we're left feeling forgotten, alone with our hurt.

Beloved, God cares about your suffering. He sees you. He knows. And He aches for you. The scriptures tell us that "God will not do wickedly" (Job 34:12 ESV). He does not bring suffering into your life; those things come from the enemy: "We know that we are from God, and the whole world lies in the power of the evil one" (1 John 5:19 ESV).

God is not only aware of your pain, but He is moved by it:

"I know their sufferings" (Exodus 3:7 ESV).
"I will be glad and rejoice in your love, for you saw my
   affliction and knew the anguish of my soul" (Psalm 31:7 NIV).
"In all their distress he too was distressed" (Isaiah 63:9 NIV).

He loves you deeply and feels your pain as if it were His own. Lean in to Jesus; He will give you strength.

This world is fallen, but God has promised that someday all our pain will be wiped away. In His eternal kingdom, suffering and death will be no more.

Father, redeem my pain for Your purpose. Amen.

Worship in Wonder

The heavens declare the glory of God, and the sky above proclaims
his handiwork. . . . Their voice goes out through all the earth, and their
words to the end of the world. In them he has set a tent for the sun.
PSALM 19:1, 4 ESV

Have you ever laid on your back under an endless blanket of glittering stars and allowed the wonder to creep into your soul? Have your thoughts drifted to the One who made it? There is a Creator God out there who designed these twinkling patterns of light for our pleasure. His greatness knows no bounds. His knowledge is complete. He knows the names He has given to each star, and He knows your name as well.

If you have never done this, grab a comfy blanket and steal out into the dark on the next clear night. Lay back and rest in awe of His eternal power. Worship Him for His limitless creativity, care, and attention to this world He called into being. Know that He knows you. The great One who drew sparkling pictures in the vastness of our universe loves you with all the greatness of His being.

Lord God, I am a small speck, like one of those pinpoints of
light among the billions, but You know my name. You know every
detail about me down to the number of hairs on my head. You see
me amid the masses. And You love me as if I were the only one. Amen.

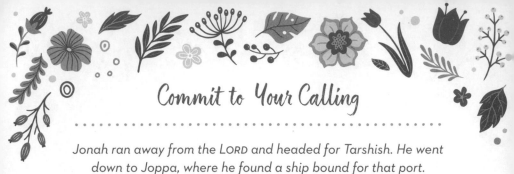

Commit to Your Calling

Jonah ran away from the LORD and headed for Tarshish. He went down to Joppa, where he found a ship bound for that port.

JONAH 1:3 NIV

Kristen felt the weight of God's nudge against her mind. She'd been ignoring it all afternoon because she was upset with her husband. They'd had an argument, and he hadn't even apologized for the things he'd said. And now God was urging *her* to apologize? Romans 12:18 (NLT) kept running through her mind like an annoying pest: "Do all that you can to live in peace with everyone." Finally she huffed out a sigh. "Okay, God, I'll go."

Jonah knew exactly what it feels like to be asked by God to do something that you don't want to do. He didn't like it, and he didn't like the people God was sending him to. It's easy to obey when what we're asked to do lines up with our own interests, but being faithful is much more difficult when obedience is costly.

God has plans for you, friend, but faithfulness to His ways is key to living in His purpose—even in the little things. Has God laid it on your heart to swallow your pride in apology, rake your grumpy neighbor's leaves, or compliment that coworker who is always criticizing you?

If you've hopped a boat that's speeding in the opposite direction, turn back now. Welcome His purpose into your life.

God, keep me committed to Your calling, no matter what. Amen.

Keep Doing Good

*Whoever sows to please the Spirit, from the Spirit will reap
eternal life. Let us not become weary in doing good, for at
the proper time we will reap a harvest if we do not give up.
Therefore, as we have opportunity, let us do good to all people,
especially to those who belong to the family of believers.*

GALATIANS 6:8–10 NIV

"Just keep swimming. Just keep swimming." We too could learn a few things by adopting the life motto of Dory, the friendly blue tang fish from the film *Finding Nemo*. Life can grind us down with its constant demands and difficult circumstances: health problems, money problems, family problems, emotional problems. Our list of trials is extensive. But we're to persevere in our purpose here—in spite of our problems.

We're here to sow seeds of faith and love and good deeds that benefit others around us. God knows a servant's heart can get tired, especially when our efforts go unnoticed and unappreciated. He encourages us through scripture: Don't get tired of doing good! Your rewards are up ahead!

Don't pass up any opportunity to do good for someone today! Don't let the enemy tell you your efforts are wasted—for you will reap an eternal harvest. Don't give up. Keep teaching your children about Jesus. Keep loving the hard to love. Keep encouraging the downhearted. Just keep swimming, friend!

Lord, may I work diligently to please Your Spirit in this life. Amen.

Knowing His Will

We do not know what we ought to pray for, but the Spirit himself intercedes for us through wordless groans. And he who searches our hearts knows the mind of the Spirit, because the Spirit intercedes for God's people in accordance with the will of God. And we know that in all things God works for the good of those who love him, who have been called according to his purpose.
ROMANS 8:26–28 NIV

My kids like to play the game "Would you rather. . . ?" Many of the options they cook up are as goofy as "Would you rather kiss a toad or lick a lizard?" But when they're deciding what to do, I use this game to give them options. All of the choices I give them would make me happy. It's their choice. If you're struggling to understand God's plan for your life, know that as a loving Father, God gives you options within His will as well—all of which are equally pleasing to Him. You choose.

Romans 8:26-28 tells us that God works for the good of *those who love Him*. If your heart is turned toward God in love and submission, He can use you in whichever option you choose. And when you're struggling with making a choice, He promises the Holy Spirit will pray for you in accordance with God's will. Love God. Walk in His Word. And His plan will be revealed day by day.

Heavenly Father, I give my decisions to You. Amen.

Near to God

*My flesh and my heart may fail, but God is the strength of my
heart and my portion forever. For behold, those who are far from
you shall perish; you put an end to everyone who is unfaithful
to you. But for me it is good to be near God; I have made the
Lord GOD my refuge, that I may tell of all your works.*

PSALM 73:26–28 ESV

Julia stepped out of her air-conditioned camper into a wall of air as thick as a wet wool blanket. She sat down in the shade, fanning herself with a magazine. Sweat trickled down her back as her red-faced toddler crawled into her lap. Hot and uncomfortable, she just wanted the presence of her mama.

Sometimes walking close with the Lord can be a little uncomfortable. He asks hard things of us. Love when you'd rather not. Exercise self-control. Wait. Be gentle. Show kindness. It's easy to look at the ungodly and think that their lives are easy, smooth-sailing fun. But God has revealed their ultimate end to us—eternal separation from Him.

The writer of Psalm 73 concluded that even though the worldly people around him seemed to be living high on the hog at the moment, he would rather be near God. We have one of two destinations: nearness with God or separation. Draw close to Him, beloved. Crawl into His lap in spite of earthly trials.

*Heavenly Father, keep me close. I desire
faithfulness over momentary fun. Amen.*

Sow Seeds of the Spirit

What a person plants, he will harvest. The person who plants
selfishness, ignoring the needs of others—ignoring God!—harvests
a crop of weeds. All he'll have to show for his life is weeds! But
the one who plants in response to God, letting God's Spirit do the
growth work in him, harvests a crop of real life, eternal life.
GALATIANS 6:7–8 MSG

Karen broke up the dirt in her front flower bed. "Mama, can I help you plant flowers?" Her son flashed a dimpled grin she could never resist. "Of course, buddy. Run and grab the white envelope of seeds off the workbench." He sprinted for the garage.

A few weeks later, Karen and her son shared a laugh when the neighbor asked why their front sidewalk was buried in a web of cucumber vines.

Both in gardening and in life, we'll reap what we sow. You can't plant seeds of selfishness and expect to harvest godliness. Want to enjoy the beautiful blossoms of a real life with God here and now and an amazing eternity with Him forever? Don't ignore God. Instead look for His movements in the world around you, and join in! Grab that pouch of seeds, and start sowing. But be sure to scatter seeds born of the Spirit: love, joy, peace, patience, kindness, goodness, faithfulness, and self-control. You won't be disappointed with your crop!

Lord, may I be conscious of my actions and attitudes.
Mold me to be more like You. Amen.

Live in His Love

The LORD your God is in your midst, a mighty one who will save;
he will rejoice over you with gladness; he will quiet you
by his love; he will exult over you with loud singing.
ZEPHANIAH 3:17 ESV

I have a daughter who's very sensitive. She gets the grumps when her daily quota of hugs isn't reached or when I haven't said enough positive words to her. But when you think about it, none of us function at full potential when we're running on an empty love tank.

We want to be wanted. We long to be loved and accepted, to belong. But the people around us are just as sin-blighted as we are. Looking for the love you desire in a rotting world will leave you unsatisfied.

But God says that He will quiet you with His love. He can soothe your anxious and wounded worry over that coworker's glare or your friend's snappish response. Because He loves you. Every last, imperfect, slightly insecure inch of you.

And when you're not laser focused on gaining the affection and acceptance of others, you see them unfiltered by your own faulty perceptions—their accusing glare could be a sign of deep hurt.

Live in His love. Don't solicit it from another inferior source. His affection is not based on our effort. He loves you because you are His—His good and masterful creation.

Lord, thank You for the soul-satisfying knowledge that I am
loved by You. Now I am free to give love away. Amen.

Longing for His Company

*Christ, having been offered once to bear the sins of many,
will appear a second time, not to deal with sin but to
save those who are eagerly waiting for him.*
HEBREWS 9:28 ESV

Have you ever missed someone so much that it became a physical ache? Their absence seems to dim the sunshine. I left a good friend at home when I went away to college. I tried to enjoy the experience of new friends and interesting classes and the thrill of being out on my own. But some of that excitement dulled in the face of my longing to be in a different place with a different person.

Do we, as believers, crave the appearance of Jesus and long for His coming with this same intensity? Paul wrote to the Philippians that "many. . . walk as enemies of the cross of Christ. Their end is destruction, their god is their belly, and they glory in their shame, with minds set on earthly things" (Philippians 3:18–19 ESV). Often we too spend most of our day distracted by earthly concerns.

But how wonderful if our thoughts are continually bent toward heaven with an attitude of expectancy. No doubt our desires for earthly pleasures and sins would fade if our longings are pinned on our desire to be in the company of our friend, our Savior.

*Jesus, I crave Your coming. I'm eagerly waiting for something so
much better than this life. I'm waiting to see Your face. Amen.*

Abide in His Rest

"Come to me, all who labor and are heavy laden, and I will give you rest. Take my yoke upon you, and learn from me, for I am gentle and lowly in heart, and you will find rest for your souls. For my yoke is easy, and my burden is light."
MATTHEW 11:28–30 ESV

Are you hopelessly running behind the train? Have the burdens and worries of this world scarred your soul with deep weariness? This world is harsh, and our problems need more than empty platitudes, such as "Tomorrow will be a better day!" Jesus offers a solution to every burden your soul strains under—He offers Himself. His formula is beautifully simplistic: "Come to me."

Jesus can take your burdens. With the power of a promise, He gives rest to souls stomped into the mud of this sin-stained world. He came to earth born as a human and proved to us that He is powerful enough to back up His word. Believe in all that He says He can do for you, and trust in His good future for you. That trust will stir the winds of hope to lift your weak soul from the slop of this world.

Come to Jesus, believe, abide in Him, and follow in His steps. You will find the soul-rest of hope.

Jesus, I believe You are the Christ. I give You my yoke in exchange for rest. Teach me to abide in You. Amen.

You've Got the Joy

Dear friends, don't be surprised at the fiery trials you are going through, as if something strange were happening to you. Instead, be very glad—for these trials make you partners with Christ in his suffering, so that you will have the wonderful joy of seeing his glory when it is revealed to all the world.

1 PETER 4:12–13 NLT

Beaten, stoned, shipwrecked, and jailed—the life of the apostle Paul sounds more like a sad country song than something to get excited about. But Paul said, "Rejoice in the Lord always; again I will say, rejoice" (Philippians 4:4 ESV).

You see, Paul knew the secret. What secret is that? "I have learned in whatever situation I am to be content. I know how to be brought low, and I know how to abound. In any and every circumstance, I have learned the secret of facing plenty and hunger, abundance and need" (Philippians 4:11–12 ESV). But the next verse is the powerhouse of his contentment: "I can do all things through him who strengthens me" (Philippians 4:13 ESV).

Jesus! The strength of Jesus fueled his contentment, and the hope of Jesus fueled his joy! Paul knew that a glorious future awaited him. So no circumstance in this life could conquer his joy. He could live in prosperity or need because though he resided here for a time, his citizenship was in heaven.

Lord, fuel my joy with the knowledge that heaven awaits! Amen.

God of Glorious Riches

*My God will supply every need of yours
according to his riches in glory in Christ Jesus.*
PHILIPPIANS 4:19 ESV

The parade was in motion. Lively tunes booming from the marching band infused the air with energy. But Holly noticed that one little girl on a float wasn't throwing any candy. She was staring forlornly into her bag. "What's wrong?" Holly asked. The little girl turned sad eyes on Holly. "I don't want to give away all the candy. I want some too." Holly smiled and pointed to several five-gallon buckets of candy and handed her a piece of taffy for her pocket. The little girl's eyes grew wide and so did her smile. She happily launched fistfuls of candy into the crowd.

Perspective is a powerful thing. Is your generosity fueled by an attitude of poverty or plenty? If you're tempted to hold back, remember that the God of the universe, who takes care of you and supplies your resources, fills your earthly basket from His limitless storehouse of glorious riches. Don't fear that God's resources are going to dry up! You can't out-give God's ability to bless you.

It's not merely money that we hoard. Be generous with your time, your love, your patience, your joy, your goodness. Give today because you are overflowing with God's bountiful blessings to you.

*Heavenly Father, fuel my generosity with the knowledge
that Your storehouse will never empty. Amen.*

Spread the Knowledge of Jesus

*Through us, he brings knowledge of Christ. Everywhere
we go, people breathe in the exquisite fragrance.
Because of Christ, we give off a sweet scent rising to God.*

2 CORINTHIANS 2:14–15 MSG

The sense of smell can seem less important than some of our other senses. For example, you'd probably rather see your friends than smell them. But smells can be powerful motivators. If you're walking through the market and you catch a whiff of delicious chocolate cake wafting from the bakery, it can stop you in your tracks. You want some of that cake!

On the flip side, bad smells can repel you. The eye-watering stench of open sewage will force you back like the opposite pole of a magnet. But beware, when the stink is masked by pleasant things, something bad can seem inviting. Some people are drawn to the aroma of a horse barn where the pungent smell of manure is mixed with the more pleasing fragrance of hay and grain. Sin can be like this too. Before you know it, you're knee-deep in something putrid.

When we do things that spread the knowledge of Jesus, it is a sweet fragrance to God. He inhales deeply the pleasant aroma of His followers who return anger with a kind word, who speak scripture to their children, who teach Sunday school classes.

*Heavenly Father, keep my feet from being
drawn to sin. In Jesus' name, amen.*

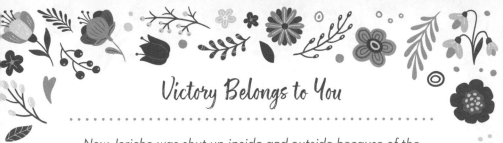

Victory Belongs to You

Now Jericho was shut up inside and outside because of the
people of Israel. None went out, and none came in. And the
LORD said to Joshua, "See, I have given Jericho into your
hand, with its king and mighty men of valor."

JOSHUA 6:1–2 ESV

The Israelites were coming off of forty hard years of desert wandering. The first time God had led them to the promised land's border, they hadn't trusted Him to deliver. Now it was time for take two. God said, "See, I have given Jericho into your hand."

He instructed them to march around the walls, blowing trumpets and shouting—easy enough if you like parades—and then the six-foot-thick walls of Jericho would fall. This time they were ready to trust. It didn't matter to God that the city was heavily fortified or that it was defended by fierce warriors. He had declared victory over the city before the walls even fell.

God may ask you to go to an intimidating place, or maybe you are in the midst of scary circumstances in your life—maybe you've lost your health, or a loved one, or your sense of security. Don't fear, beloved. God is already there ahead of you. And Jesus has declared victory over your life. Trust Him today. Walk in obedience to His Word, and victory is yours.

Lord, Your ability to do what You say is absolute.
Give me greater trust. Amen.

Speak His Words

"So is my word that goes out from my mouth: It will not return to me empty, but will accomplish what I desire and achieve the purpose for which I sent it."

ISAIAH 55:11 NIV

"Sticks and stones may break my bones, but words will never hurt me." We've all heard this adage and can testify from personal experience to its inaccuracy. Words have power. Our words have the positive power to build up another's confidence and sense of well-being, but they also have the destructive force to tear down, degrade, shame, and criticize.

God demonstrated the stunning creative power of His words in the Garden of Eden when He spoke and the world snapped into existence from the void. And Jesus is called the Word—the creative force of God's voice. When God speaks, people are changed.

If you believe that Jesus came to this earth to redeem you from the darkness, forgive your sins, and save your eternal soul, you belong to God. You are indwelt with His Holy Spirit. He wants you to listen for His still, small voice and for you to speak His words. Instead of judgment and criticism that destroy both your family and your family of believers, speak Spirit-inspired words that build up, encourage, and comfort those around you. Ask the Holy Spirit to speak His uplifting words into your life today.

*Lord, I'm listening for Your Spirit.
Speak words of life to me. Amen.*

Walk in His Power

He said to me, "My grace is sufficient for you, for my power is made perfect in weakness." Therefore I will boast all the more gladly of my weaknesses, so that the power of Christ may rest upon me.

2 CORINTHIANS 12:9 ESV

You may think that God cannot use you, that the brokenness that litters your past disqualifies you or that your weaknesses render you ineffective. But those are Satan's lies to you. Mother Teresa said this: "I am a little pencil in God's hands. He does the thinking. He does the writing. He does everything and sometimes it is really hard because it is a broken pencil and He has to sharpen it a little more."[10]

Friend, you're giving your flaws too much credit. The living God of the universe is bigger than whatever weakness is debilitating you. God has all the power. And He told the apostle Paul, "My power is made perfect in weakness." Be the pencil. The pencil does nothing but wait, ready for use. It can take no credit for the words written by the one who holds it.

Yes, we are weak. Yes, we are flawed. But we are not without hope. We are not unusable. Share about your limitations, and experience the power of Christ as the Holy Spirit accomplishes God's work through you, all the more gloriously because of your weakness.

God, I give You myself. I can do nothing on my own.
May I move in Your power. Amen.

---

[10] Jaya Chaliha and Edward Le Joly, comps., *The Joy in Loving: A Guide to Daily Living with Mother Teresa* (New York: Penguin, 1996), 276.

Protection from Pride

I know a man in Christ who fourteen years ago was caught up to the third heaven—whether in the body or out of the body I do not know, God knows. And I know that this man was caught up into paradise. . . and he heard things that cannot be told, which man may not utter. . . . So to keep me from becoming conceited because of the surpassing greatness of the revelations, a thorn was given me in the flesh.
2 CORINTHIANS 12:2-4, 7 ESV

The apostle Paul was given an extravagant revelation—he experienced the paradise of heaven! He heard things so great he wasn't permitted to share them. How exciting! His experience was so awesome that God had to keep his head from swelling. So God gave him a thorn. Something to wake him up to the reality of his circumstances—a sinful human in need of Jesus.

Humility is seeing yourself clearly. If you stay in touch with your limitations, you won't be tempted to think a bit too much of yourself. Jesus said, "Blessed [spiritually prosperous, happy, to be admired] are the poor in spirit [those devoid of spiritual arrogance, those who regard themselves as insignificant], for theirs is the kingdom of heaven [both now and forever]" (Matthew 5:3 AMP). We cannot enter into God's kingdom without recognizing our need for Him. How can your limitations lead you into a renewed humility and dependence on God?

Father, forgive me if I have operated in pride. Amen.

Face-to-Face Encounter

"For this is the covenant that I will make with the house of Israel after those days, declares the L<small>ORD</small>: I will put my law within them, and I will write it on their hearts. And I will be their God, and they shall be my people. And no longer shall each one teach his neighbor and each his brother, saying, 'Know the L<small>ORD</small>,' for they shall all know me, from the least of them to the greatest, declares the L<small>ORD</small>. For I will forgive their iniquity, and I will remember their sin no more."

JEREMIAH 31:33–34 ESV

You can know God! You can have a personal relationship with Him when you receive His Holy Spirit. Becoming a believer is not about following rules carved in stone. It's loving a living God who loves you back and doing life with Him. "Whenever, though, they turn to face God as Moses did, God removes the veil and there they are—face-to-face! They suddenly recognize that God is a living, personal presence, not a piece of chiseled stone" (2 Corinthians 3:16–17 MSG).

Talk to Him. Spend time in His presence. Read about Him in His Word. Still yourself, and listen for His voice. He wants conversation and participation in your life. "Those who trust God's action in them find that God's Spirit is in them—living and breathing God!" (Romans 8:5 MSG).

*Holy Spirit, I invite You to speak to
me today. In Jesus' name, amen.*

Love Letter

You show that you are a letter from Christ delivered by us,
written not with ink but with the Spirit of the living God,
not on tablets of stone but on tablets of human hearts.

2 CORINTHIANS 3:3 ESV

Receiving letters is fun. Eye-catching stationery or a beautifully illustrated card fills you with a special sense of significance that someone would take time to pause the rush of their life to pen words meant just for you. Whether they're sharing news from their world or sending you a note of encouragement or thanks, it means a lot to hold that tangible evidence of your worth to them—to know your well-being takes up space in their thoughts.

The Bible says that *you* are a letter too! A letter from Christ penned by the Holy Spirit to everyone you come in contact with. God's Spirit is written on your heart. He wants His transforming power to spill out of you in encouragement and hope just as the welcome words of a dear friend's letter. His life is written on your life!

What words are penned by the way you are living? Does Jesus' love, grace, and kindness speak from your attitudes and actions in a fervent letter to His beloved? If not, ask Him to transform you into a love letter to the world—one bursting with the tender hope of every person's worth in His eyes.

Jesus, may my life be living proof of Your
regenerating love. In Jesus' name, amen.

Transformed in Glory

*Whenever anyone turns to the Lord, the veil is taken away. Now the
Lord is the Spirit, and where the Spirit of the Lord is, there is freedom.
And we all, who with unveiled faces contemplate the Lord's glory,
are being transformed into his image with ever-increasing glory,
which comes from the Lord, who is the Spirit.*

2 Corinthians 3:16–18 niv

The moon owns no light of its own, yet it shines into the dark pitch of night. Its face merely beholds the sun's brightness and reflects its borrowed light.

Jesus has ripped away the shroud of our broken relationship with God: "Let us come boldly to the throne of our gracious God" (Hebrews 4:16 nlt). We now live in the freedom of His life—the freedom to behold His glory and to walk with Him again in conversation, the freedom to experience a transformation!

This change isn't a one-time event. Instead we become more like His image with ever-increasing glory! "I am certain that God, who began the good work within you, will continue his work until it is finally finished on the day when Christ Jesus returns" (Philippians 1:6 nlt).

Allow the Holy Spirit's adept and gentle hands to continuously mold the contours of your character. His bright presence will shine from your countenance and pierce this world's dark cloak of brokenness, sin, and pain.

*God, as I look upon Your glory, change me. May my soul shine
radiantly with the borrowed brightness of Your Son. Amen.*

Kindness Counts

When the goodness and loving kindness of God our Savior appeared, he saved us, not because of works done by us in righteousness, but according to his own mercy, by the washing of regeneration and renewal of the Holy Spirit, whom he poured out on us richly through Jesus Christ our Savior.

TITUS 3:4–6 ESV

A friend gives you a book or shows up to help you paint your living room. Or better yet, a stranger pays for your meal, just because. Are you surprised by this person's kindness? Shocked by unexpected goodness?

Most people survive their stint here with a narrow self-focus on their own affairs and schedules. So when someone goes out of their way to do something nice, people are arrested by their kindness. They pause at the simple act of a selfless deed and wonder at its root, *Why would you do that for me?* Especially when a stranger is the recipient of someone's unsolicited generosity of spirit.

Jesus does the same for you, my friend. He saved you by the most shocking act of kindness ever: He was whipped and mocked and spat upon, and His hands and feet were pierced with nails—He died in your place. Now it falls to you to carry on His work. Arrest someone today with the kindness of Jesus. Lock them in the magnetic power of His goodness. They will gravitate to His grace and be transformed by His truth.

Lord, lead me to the acts of kindness
You have planned for me today. Amen.

Courage to Speak

"For if you keep silent at this time, relief and deliverance will rise for the Jews from another place, but you and your father's house will perish. And who knows whether you have not come to the kingdom for such a time as this?"

ESTHER 4:14 ESV

Mia pulled open the glass door of the café, and Claire instantly felt a familiar knot tighten in her gut. Mia was a nice-enough girl, but she always had something to "share" about someone. Maybe she thought of it as news, but Claire squirmed as the personal details of other people's lives spread like spilled milk across the table. She'd hoped that maybe Mia would miss coffee this morning because she always felt a little grimy afterward. But what could she do?

Have you ever watched a wrong play out in front of you but done nothing to right it or prevent it from happening? Or maybe you did say something but were then criticized or ostracized from the group. God has strategically positioned you in your exact life. Just as Esther had to choose whether she would stand up or shut up, so do we. Whether it's the hurtful injustice of sharing gossip or the mass tragedy of countless abortions, how do you know that you weren't put in your corner of earth for such a time as this? Will you remain silent?

Heavenly Father, give me wisdom and courage to speak the truth—but always tempered by love. Amen.

Generous in Every Way

God can pour on the blessings in astonishing ways so that you're ready for anything and everything, more than just ready to do what needs to be done. As one psalmist puts it, He throws caution to the winds, giving to the needy in reckless abandon. His right-living, right-giving ways never run out, never wear out. This most generous God who gives seed to the farmer that becomes bread for your meals is more than extravagant with you. He gives you something you can then give away, which grows into full-formed lives, robust in God, wealthy in every way, so that you can be generous in every way, producing with us great praise to God.

2 CORINTHIANS 9:8–11 MSG

Mine. Mine. Mine. Sadly it's a mantra that's heard not just in preschool classrooms. Do you tend to think of the blessings God gives you as yours? Instead of tightly holding your gifts from God, try resting those blessings on open palms.

Generally we're sharers or hoarders. Do you give freely of what you have? It might be spending time to help out a friend (or a stranger!) or to really listen to what others say when they speak. Or it could be money, food, a skill that you have, spiritual wisdom you've gained, clothes you don't wear (or even some you do!). God is extravagant with you! Pay it forward, and profit great praise to God!

*Father, may Your freehanded blessings
pass through me to others. Amen.*

Doers

Be doers of the word, and not hearers only, deceiving yourselves. For if anyone is a hearer of the word and not a doer, he is like a man who looks intently at his natural face in a mirror. For he looks at himself and goes away and at once forgets what he was like. But the one who looks into the perfect law, the law of liberty, and perseveres, being no hearer who forgets but a doer who acts, he will be blessed in his doing.
JAMES 1:22–25 ESV

It's easy to have a double standard for your behavior. Do you act super sweet in public and release the real you when no one's looking—the one who can be a real rotten peach?

We all have bad days, ones where our peachy attitudes take a sour turn. But don't allow that phase to become your lifestyle. Integrity is doing what we know is right, even when no one is watching. Is your integrity intact?

We can't hide even our secret thoughts from God. He knows all of our motives, attitudes, and actions. God sees the real you and loves you still. In fact, He loves you too much to leave you where you are! That's why He's working to make you more like Jesus.

Lord, make me into the daughter You desire. Help me be a doer of Your Word even when no one else is looking. Amen.

Clean Up My Heart

Create in me a clean heart, O God,
and renew a right spirit within me.
PSALM 51:10 ESV

You push up from your aching knees to admire your mop job. Your kitchen floor catches the sunlight streaming through your windows and sparkles. You lean against the counter for just a moment to bask in your accomplishment. But just as you push off the counter's edge to put away your cleaning bucket, the back door slams open. Your son and his dog both tromp mud across your glossy floor. You open your mouth to scold, but only a sigh escapes. Later your daughter's spaghetti slips off her fork and splats on the floor, followed by a waterfall of milk from her overturned cup. Cleaning can be an endless and thankless cycle.

Thankfully God is not wearied by the daily housekeeping chore of shining up our hearts. He never tires of setting things right in our spirits. When poor attitudes, selfishness, or unforgiveness stomp muddy prints through the halls of our freshly washed hearts, He's ready to scrub the mess with a mop sprinkled in conviction and grace.

Day after day we try to keep our lives pure, but each day we end up soiled in some puddle of sin. We can't make our hearts pristine, but He can!

Thank You, God, that You are steadfast in Your love for me.
May my love for You be just as unwavering. Amen.

Bring Peace

*Walk in a manner worthy of the calling to which you have been called,
with all humility and gentleness, with patience, bearing with one another
in love, eager to maintain the unity of the Spirit in the bond of peace.*
EPHESIANS 4:1–3 ESV

Natalie could not be silent any longer. She marched down the hall toward her meeting, her anger roiling. *That* woman had criticized every change Natalie had implemented with the children's program. She'd complained about the music, the snacks, the curriculum—yet hadn't lifted a finger to help in any way. Natalie paused outside the door for a final gasp of air before plunging into enemy waters. The Sunday school bulletin board caught her eye. The words she read splashed cool living water over her searing anger: "Blessed are the peacemakers, for they shall be called sons of God" (Matthew 5:9 ESV).

People are a messy business. Jesus knew this well. He dealt with His share of hypocrites, angry criticism, and injustice. Yet He came to this world to offer us peace—the peace of God that surpasses all understanding, the peace of forgiveness, grace, and new life, not anger and judgment. The Son of God calls us into our inheritance as children of God by following in His steps as peacemakers. When you're tempted to react in anger, remember whose child you are. Meet discord with the humility, gentleness, patience, and the love of Christ.

*Heavenly Father, help me to bring peace in
gentleness and not an angry response. Amen.*

Forgive

*"Whenever you stand praying, forgive, if you have
anything against anyone, so that your Father also
who is in heaven may forgive you your trespasses."*

MARK 11:25 ESV

Forgive. The word echoed through her mind in response to Hannah's desperate prayer. But how could she? The hurt cut so deep. Her anger felt justified and satisfying to her wounded spirit. The damage inflicted on her was an awful thing. Was she just supposed to forget it? Forgive and forget—isn't that what people said? Obviously they'd never been so grievously injured by another person. Scourged by vicious tongues. Pierced by undeserved punishment. Who could possibly forgive that?

Beloved, maybe you've been abandoned or hurt by those who were supposed to love you. That kind of pain can leave you leery of trusting again. Anger and bitterness can find purchase in your torn-up soul. But there is hope. Forgiveness is possible. Someone else was betrayed by friends, whipped, and beaten. His body was pierced by nails, and He gave up His life for you. In the midst of His anguished body and soul, He cried out, "Father, forgive them" (Luke 23:34 ESV).

And He also forgives you. In Christ we can forgive much because we have been forgiven everything. Rest your war-torn mind. His righteous judgment will come in His time. He hasn't overlooked you. God says, "It is mine to avenge; I will repay" (Hebrews 10:30 NIV). His justice will reign. Release it to God. Forgive, and find peace.

Lord, bring true forgiveness and healing to my heart. Amen.

Through His Eyes

*"You are precious in my eyes,
and honored, and I love you."*
ISAIAH 43:4 ESV

A beggar extends a grimy hand of acceptance as you offer him a steaming cup of coffee, but his eyes don't quite meet yours as he mumbles his thanks. An angry little girl in a torn dress and ratty pigtails swears defiantly at you on the playground when you catch her kicking other kids. An elderly woman can no longer remember your name, even though you call her Mom.

God sees the same word etched across the broken surface of every life—*precious*. Each and every one matters to Him. He suffers with the pain of their heartaches. He cares about the burdens they stumble beneath. He longs for their presence in His kingdom. He treasures their soul with the same tenderness He gives to yours.

Circumstances in this world may have been more kind to you than others—or maybe not. Whether this world deems you as valuable or worthless, your Father in heaven has better names for you: precious, unique, beloved, worthy, forgiven, pure. He calls you daughter.

*Heavenly Father, give me fresh eyes. Give me Your eyes
so I can see others as You do. In Jesus' name, amen.*

Conqueror

"Behold, I have given you authority to tread on serpents and scorpions, and over all the power of the enemy, and nothing shall hurt you."
LUKE 10:19 ESV

Kara headed for bed. But after taking two steps into the living room, she jerked her bare toes back from a sharp jab. Legos. She strategically tiptoed through the rest of the Lego land mines, feeling for tiny sharp blocks. Victory! She dragged her fatigued legs up the darkened stairs only to trip over a smiling stuffed penguin. The jaunty strains of "Jingle Bells" cracked the silence. Kara grabbed the handrail for support against further surprise attacks.

As a child of God, you have an enemy in this world whose traps for you aren't innocently or carelessly left behind. No, you have the worst kind of enemy—one who knows you. He has been studying human nature for a very long time, and He has an arsenal of tricks to draw you away from God. He sets you up. And he wants to take you out—out of peace, out of freedom, out of God's plans, and out of life everlasting.

But don't fear, brave friend. Satan is also predictable. He's a liar. And the only way to combat lies is with truth. Study God's Word. Memorize His truth and know your enemy. Learn Satan's strategy so you won't be caught in his snares. And know this: "We are more than conquerors through him who loved us" (Romans 8:37 ESV).

Lord, give me wisdom to avoid Satan's traps. Amen.

Pause to Listen

"My sheep listen to my voice;
I know them, and they follow me."

JOHN 10:27 NIV

Piper's mind wandered from the story her friend Brooke was sharing. She was forgetting something from her grocery list, and it danced at the fringe of her memory. Her mom had a doctor's appointment the next day, and she was worried about her test results. Oh, and her husband needed a shirt ironed for his big meeting. And she wanted to tell Brooke about her ideas for VBS before she left.

"Isn't that a great idea, Piper?" Brooke was smiling at her with wide eyes and arched brows. Oops. Piper really hadn't meant to tune out her friend.

How intently do we listen for God's voice during our day or even during our quiet time? Slowing the raging river of our thoughts feels like an impossible task at times. But how are we ever to participate in God's plans for our day if we don't stop to hear His words?

Try a new prayer strategy today—listen more and talk less. God does care about all of your needs and problems, but often our prayers devolve into a lengthy laundry list of wants and worries. The Creator of the universe, the mighty God of heaven, has plans for you today. Pause the patter of your spilling words and wait. Be still. Be silent. Listen. Welcome His input into your conversation.

Lord, teach me to listen for Your voice
in the moments of my day. Amen.

Come Closer

Since we have confidence to enter the holy places by the blood of Jesus, by the new and living way that he opened for us through the curtain, that is, through his flesh, and since we have a great priest over the house of God, let us draw near with a true heart in full assurance of faith, with our hearts sprinkled clean from an evil conscience and our bodies washed with pure water. Let us hold fast the confession of our hope without wavering, for he who promised is faithful.

HEBREWS 10:19–23 ESV

The sunshine pulls you. It woos you outside into its warm embrace. You close your eyes and tilt your face up to receive its gentle kiss on your skin. A sigh escapes, and your muscles mold into your deck chair like warm wax. A smile touches your lips, and your worries seem to melt away.

Jesus is the brilliant, shining sun to this dark and troubled world. His love is magnetic. And through Him we find hope. Hope for our future. Hope for our present. Hope for our families. Hope for our problems. Hope through our failures.

Step out of the cold shadows and into His light. Energize your tired and chilly soul in the sunshine of His promises. Come in from the cold. You don't have to do this life alone.

Jesus, draw me closer. I'm holding on tight to my hope in You because You are faithful. Amen.

All-Powerful Jesus

"I lay down my life that I may take it up again. No one takes it from me, but I lay it down of my own accord. I have authority to lay it down, and I have authority to take it up again."

JOHN 10:17–18 ESV

How do you recognize people with authority? Is it the power suits they wear? Their haircuts? While those things can make a great impression, if there's no action behind the look they've achieved, their positions are pretty meaningless. When someone with authority speaks, things happen. When the boss enters the room, everyone jumps to the task at hand.

We can rest easy knowing that Jesus has authority. In heaven and in earth, Jesus can make things happen. He's no frail Savior. Don't get the wrong idea that just because He was nailed to a cross that His power and authority were ever in question. No, those soldiers didn't kill Jesus on that cross. The Lord of the universe laid down His life—willingly. For me. For you.

This is the same Jesus who stilled a violent storm with a few words. The same Jesus who commanded demons. This Jesus had authority both to lay down His life and to pick it back up again three days later and walk out of a tomb. This is your Jesus too. The almighty, powerful Jesus who loves you.

Heavenly Father, thank You for the resurrection—the evidence that You have all the power! In Jesus' name, amen.

Beautiful One

The Mighty One, God the LORD, speaks and summons the earth from the rising of the sun to its setting. Out of Zion, the perfection of beauty, God shines forth. Our God comes; he does not keep silence; before him is a devouring fire, around him a mighty tempest.

PSALM 50:1–3 ESV

Celeste relaxed in the golden glow of sunset. Orange and pink streaked across the sky, igniting the clouds and then fading from purple to deep blue. She reveled in the knowledge that this sunset was a singular event painted just for this day by her Creator. Never again would the wonder of this particular day's fiery close be seen. In the glorious riot of colors, she recognized the beauty of God's nature and the brilliance of His glory.

God's work brings forth beauty not only around us but in us as well. His nature is beauty, so He cannot help but birth more beauty around Him and in those in which His very Spirit dwells. He desires the imperishable beauty of a gentle and quiet spirit in us. May your life be infused with grace, gentleness, and peace. May you be an image bearer of His beauty today.

Father, we can't look on Your glory. And the brilliance of a sunset is only a vague reflection of Your glorious beauty. May I bear the image of even a small portion of Your love, Your grace, and Your beautiful Spirit today. Amen.

Alive in Him

*You also must consider yourselves dead
to sin and alive to God in Christ Jesus.*

ROMANS 6:11 ESV

Jesus had been executed. The women, Mary Magdalene, Mary the mother of James, and Salome, had gone to the tomb early Sunday morning with spices to anoint the body of Jesus. They were surely in despair. What was happening? Their Jesus had been killed. It must have seemed surreal. Had it been a fairy tale? Was He not who He said He was?

When the women arrived at the tomb, they found the stone rolled away and Jesus' body was gone! While they were wondering about this, two men stood beside them in dazzling clothes. "Why do you seek the living among the dead? He is not here, but has risen" (Luke 24:5-6 ESV).

Our sight sometimes gets hung up on "dead" things too. We forget what God has said and return to old sins and habits that lead only to death, just as the women did not remember that Jesus said He would rise. But Jesus has delivered us from death into new life. He has taken the punishment of hell for us and conquered death. He came through it and stepped out of the tomb alive! Drop your old dead things and embrace godly habits that lead to life. Live like you are alive in Him!

*Jesus, You delivered me from death. You satisfied
heaven's justice for me. Help me live for You. Amen.*

Kindness Is Cool

"I tell you, love your enemies. Help and give without expecting a return. You'll never—I promise—regret it. Live out this God-created identity the way our Father lives toward us, generously and graciously, even when we're at our worst. Our Father is kind; you be kind."

LUKE 6:35–36 MSG

That's it! The perfect comeback. The zinger you've been rehearsing in your head for a week is now poised on the tip of your tongue. That woman has irritated you for the last time, and you've had enough. You're ready to blast her with a piece of your mind and put her in her place. You're already anticipating your smug satisfaction in knowing you let her have what she deserved.

But will you feel satisfied? Or will remorse inevitably follow in the wake of Miss Nasty? Most likely instead of feeling gratified, you'll spend the remainder of your week wishing for the chance to snatch back that moment and curb your tongue.

Wouldn't it be better to be kind? To become a cool and soothing presence in a world as angry and irritated as a porcupine with poison ivy? Kindness definitely comes with less cringe-worthy strings attached! Serve out an extra measure of grace and kindness when you encounter hostility and crankiness—just like Jesus does for you.

Lord, guard my words. My demeanor and behavior are a reflection of the One I belong to—You, Jesus. Amen.

Fear Not!

*"Are not two sparrows sold for a penny? And not one
of them will fall to the ground apart from your Father."*
MATTHEW 10:29 ESV

Your child cries out in the night. A nightmare. She's trembling with fear from imaginary monsters. You hug her tight and assure her that you're there and she has nothing to fear. Monsters aren't real, and she can sleep in peace.

But as we grow older, we realize that while the bogeyman is a figment of our scared childhood mind, this world does hold some real, live monsters. Horrible things do sometimes happen, and evil does exist. But Jesus offers hope. He confronted the darkness of this world and said, "Do not fear those who kill the body but cannot kill the soul. Rather fear him who can destroy both soul and body in hell" (Matthew 10:28 ESV). In other words, Jesus says, "The only one you should be afraid of is Me."

Jesus holds all the cards. The power of eternal life is in His hands. "Fear not, therefore; you are of more value than many sparrows. So everyone who acknowledges me before men, I also will acknowledge before my Father who is in heaven" (Matthew 10:31–32 ESV). Do you know Him? Do you call Him friend? Can you rest today in the peace of His promise?

*Jesus, thank You that I don't have to fear even death
because my eternal future is secure in You. Amen.*

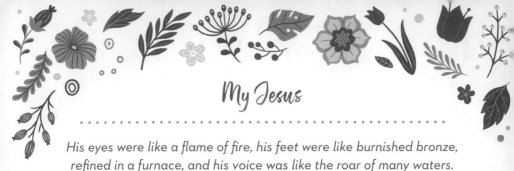

My Jesus

His eyes were like a flame of fire, his feet were like burnished bronze,
refined in a furnace, and his voice was like the roar of many waters.
REVELATION 1:14–15 ESV

Some people put God in the same category as the Easter Bunny. A little magical, maybe a bit fantastical, but ultimately soft and cuddly. But in Revelation, John was terrified by the blindingly bright Being he saw with flaming eyes and a double-edged sword for a tongue.

Until the shining One laid His hand on John and said, "Fear not, I am the first and the last, and the living one" (Revelation 1:17–18 ESV). Then John realized—*Oh, it's my Jesus!*

Consider the great, wonderful, amazing, and awe-inducing power of the living God of the universe. Spend some time contemplating just what God is capable of. Because if you don't know the power of God, then you will be afraid of what life may throw at you. You will fear death, illness, the future, or what's going to happen to your kids. Don't live a life of fear. Read the opening chapter of Revelation and see Jesus unmasked. He's no fuzzy bunny, my friend. But He is still your Jesus.

What kind of Jesus are you serving? Is He timid and fluffy or powerful and frightening to His enemies?

Jesus, You are the mighty One who walked through
death for me and came out alive. Wipe away my
fears of this life as I live in Your power. Amen.

When Mountains Crumble

*God is our refuge and strength, always ready to help in times
of trouble. So we will not fear when earthquakes come and
the mountains crumble into the sea. . . . The LORD of Heaven's
Armies is here among us; the God of Israel is our fortress.*
PSALM 46:1–2, 7 NLT

Emily glanced into the bathroom—and paused. The sink was smeared with sticky pink blobs of toothpaste. Were they painting with it? Sheesh! And did they have to spray the mirror with spit *every* time they brushed their teeth? And the wet towels—yes, that's towels, *plural*, because apparently one giant fluffy towel wasn't sufficient—lay heaped on the rug. Right. Under. The. Hooks. Emily came unglued. She screamed at her kids. She demanded they clean the entire bathroom this instant. And amid their red eyes and tear-stained cheeks, the guilt assaulted her.

Have you been to this place, friend? Sometimes our emotions bushwhack us. They build until the rising pressure forces an eruption of volcanic proportions. We spew destruction, often hurting the ones we love best. But God has promised to be our refuge through much bigger problems than a dirty sink. He promises to be your refuge even if the mountains fall into the sea. Today, ask God to take your struggle with anger and fear and use it to bring new life and strength instead of destruction.

*Father, help me sort out my raw emotions.
Show me how to take baby steps into new life. Amen.*

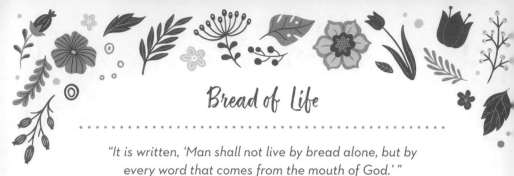

Bread of Life

"It is written, 'Man shall not live by bread alone, but by every word that comes from the mouth of God.'"

MATTHEW 4:4 ESV

Jesus had been fasting in the wilderness for forty days. He had to be getting desperately hungry because I can't even make it to lunch without fantasizing about food—my thoughts have me taking a sharp left toward the kitchen while my mouth waters. Satan zeroed in on Jesus' weak spot and mocked Him—if He was the Son of God, He should just turn some stones into bread.

Raise your hand if you've skipped over Deuteronomy in your read-the-Bible-in-a-year plan. Raise your hand if you have trouble pronouncing Deuteronomy. It's okay, friend. I've been there too. But a quick peek at how Jesus turned back Satan's temptations might have you taking a closer look at this book. Every time Jesus quoted Deuteronomy.

And this time He said something like, "Do you think that mere bread can sustain your life? Live on a steady diet of the words from God's mouth."

Jesus says eat bread and live for a day. Eat the Word of God, chew on it, internalize it until it becomes enmeshed in the fiber of your being—and you will truly live. Not just for today, but forever. Forever, my friend! Crack open the Word, and find a better life, a deeper life, a more fulfilling life—an everlasting life.

God, may I read Your words—and live! Amen.

Moving Up

"He will wipe away every tear from their eyes, and death shall be no more, neither shall there be mourning, nor crying, nor pain anymore, for the former things have passed away."

REVELATION 21:4 ESV

You move into a starter home when you graduate college and get your first job. It's small, has a few cosmetic issues, and a cracked sidewalk. The neighborhood is less than upscale and a bit outdated. But you dream about moving up. You plan your perfect home and sketch out its rooms.

When the burdens of this life threaten to break you, remember that this world is not your forever home. Life here has its patched plaster and foundation cracks. Or maybe it has left you feeling like a gutted fixer-upper. But don't despair in your current circumstances. Jesus knows how hard this life can hit. He was beaten up by it too.

But this is not the end of your house hunt. Jesus is right now with the Father, getting your new place ready for you. And none of the things that trouble us here will follow us there. Think about it! The Creator of this planet is designing a home for you. It's exciting. It's custom built. And I doubt He used all His best stuff on this temporary place. Just wait and see! It's going to be jaw-dropping.

Lord, no more tears, no more pain or sins,
no more death to worry about. I can hardly
imagine how wonderful it will be with You! Amen.

Lesson in Service

"He who is least among you all
is the one who is great."
LUKE 9:48 ESV

In Jesus' day people walked along dusty and manure-speckled roads in sandals. By evening their feet surely smelled less than floral. It was the job of the lowest servant in the house to wash the feet of all the guests before they reclined around a dinner table together. After all, no one wants dirty feet served up next to their salad.

When Jesus and the disciples sat down for the Passover meal, no one offered to scrub feet, perhaps because they'd already been caught arguing about who was going to be the greatest in Jesus' kingdom.

So Jesus took off His shirt, grabbed a towel and a basin, and began to wash the dirt from their feet. Jesus. The Son of God. The Creator of the universe. The Alpha and Omega. The One with no beginning and no end, knelt and took up the job of the lowest servant. The disciples had to have cringed, thinking, *I should be the one doing this! Not Jesus.* But Jesus then said they were to follow His example.

Is your heart for service? Do you reach out in love—or complain? Our communities and our churches should be better because we are in them. Roll up your sleeves and ask, "How can I help?"

Jesus, teach me to have a humble heart.
Teach me to serve. Amen.

Be Known by Your Love

Suppose a brother or a sister is without clothes and daily food. If one of you says to them, "Go in peace; keep warm and well fed," but does nothing about their physical needs, what good is it? In the same way, faith by itself, if it is not accompanied by action, is dead.

JAMES 2:15–17 NIV

How can we measure our devotion to Jesus? Is it the size of our Bibles? The number of times we attend church services on any given week? The amount of money we place in the offering plate? By tattooing the object of our affection right on our skin? Will Jesus ink mean that I'm a more devoted follower of Christ?

Please understand: the mark of Jesus is not a tattoo. But He did tell His disciples exactly what His mark on their lives would look like: "All people will know that you are my disciples, if you have love for one another" (John 13:35 ESV). The whole world will know you by your love.

Jesus cared about people. He saw their problems and ached for them. He reached out to them with healing and forgiveness and compassion. He loved them. Does your love for the struggling people of this world mark you as His?

Heavenly Father, I want to be known as Yours.
Place Your mark of love upon my life. Amen.

Growing Up

*Practice these things, immerse yourself in them,
so that all may see your progress.*

1 TIMOTHY 4:15 ESV

We diligently chart our children's growth from infancy. The instant they stand we mark off their height inside a door frame and marvel at their added inches every year. Each new skill they learn and every goal they reach is noted and applauded. But what if they failed to grow? What if they remained content with crawling and simply refused to walk? What if grunting satisfied their need to communicate and they never acquired the skill of speech? That would be a tragedy. A life stunted. A potential lost.

But what about our spiritual growth? Many followers of Jesus are living stunted, disabled spiritual lives because they've grown comfortable with their developmental stage. Paul told the Corinthians he had to address them as infants in Christ and feed them milk because they weren't ready for the meat of God's Word. He said, "While there is jealousy and strife among you, are you not of the flesh and behaving only in a human way?" (1 Corinthians 3:3 ESV). In Hebrews we're encouraged to "leave the elementary doctrine of Christ and go on to maturity" (Hebrews 6:1 ESV).

Beloved, don't continue crawling when you were meant to run. Cultivate a hunger for the deep things of God. Follow the leading of the Holy Spirit. Study His Word. Learn His ways. You don't want to miss out on the fullness of His breathtaking plans!

Father, teach me something new about You today. Amen.

Come Back to Him

If I say, "Surely the darkness shall cover me, and the light about me be night," even the darkness is not dark to you; the night is bright as the day, for darkness is as light with you.

PSALM 139:11–12 ESV

Adele noticed a crumpled candy wrapper on the floor and a bare foot poking out from behind a chair. She pressed her lips together to squelch a smile when that same little bare foot began tapping a happy rhythm on the floor. She quietly leaned over the back of the chair and peered down into the narrow space behind it. "I see you." The tapping stopped. Her little girl tilted a chocolate-covered face up to reveal round blue eyes. "Mama, how did you find me?"

Have you attempted to hide from God like Adam and Eve? Or run from Him like Jonah? It seems we're all prone to repeat the same ridiculous behavior when being disobedient. It's irrational to think we can give God the slip or dodge His all-seeing glance. It's like running from your shadow. You will never escape. He knows exactly where you are and what you are doing there. Yet He calls out as He did in the Garden of Eden: "Where are you?" (Genesis 3:9 ESV)

Will you answer Him today? Will you step back into the light of His forgiveness?

Father, I'm so sorry. I didn't want You to see me, but You already know. Please forgive me, and help me to live righteously. Amen.

What's Your Story?

But God chose what is foolish in the world to shame the wise; God chose what is weak in the world to shame the strong; God chose what is low and despised in the world, even things that are not, to bring to nothing things that are, so that no human being might boast in the presence of God.

God doesn't want to erase your experiences. He's not a God of waste. He is a God of creativity. Your utter failures, your crushing defeats, your hardships and hurts—He doesn't sweep up the shattered pieces and toss them in a wastebasket. He doesn't fetch a pristine piece of clay to mold. Instead He gathers all those precious shards: each jagged corner, every splintered, irregular shape. He spreads them gently before Him and fits them together into something new, something unexpected, something beautiful.

Loved ones, don't despair if sin has left you fractured and fragile. You are not unusable. You are not wasted. You are not garbage. Things that drove you to your knees and broke you can bring you to Jesus. Offer Him your broken life. In the hands of the Master, from what once appeared as nothing more than shattered glass, a stunning mosaic will emerge. Your broken pieces tell a story that He can use. And He wants your story for His glory!

Lord, take my life. Take my story. Use it to encourage and draw someone to You today. Amen.

Slow Down

*My dear brothers and sisters, take note of this: Everyone should
be quick to listen, slow to speak and slow to become angry.*

JAMES 1:19 NIV

"Quick to listen, slow to speak and slow to become angry." This admonition suggests James was well acquainted with the emotional creatures called humans. Surely he arranged his words strategically because he knew that the opposite is usually true. We don't listen. We spew thoughtless words. We misunderstand and we get mad. He knew that our humanity is prone to run after the wrong things. Our emotions are too often poised on the starting block, set to anticipate the worst. And our tongue is quickest off the block when anger fires off the starting shot.

But what if we listened more carefully? What if your next conversation wasn't about you? What if you chose to believe that the best possible intentions are behind any potentially upsetting comments that come your way? Maybe they were even intended for your good. The next time you hear potentially upsetting comments, take the slow road—slow to overreact, slow to anger. A simple question to clarify their words might just save you a whole lot of stewing in bitter juices.

*Lord, help me weigh my words today before I speak them.
Give me the patience to listen and the wisdom to
choose truth over irrational anger. Amen.*

Experience God's Fullness

That you, being rooted and grounded in love, may have strength to comprehend with all the saints what is the breadth and length and height and depth, and to know the love of Christ that surpasses knowledge, that you may be filled with all the fullness of God.

 EPHESIANS 3:17–19 ESV

The room is crowded. Laughter and conversation float through the relaxed atmosphere. But your nerves are strung tighter than a piano string. Small groups of people chat easily, but you don't know a single one. Your head tells you to go and introduce yourself, but you can't coax up enough courage to interrupt their conversations. Is everyone too self-absorbed to even notice you?

We've all been there and had that feeling of being on the outside. But is someone else really at fault? Or is your internal need for acceptance driving you?

In Ephesians 3, Paul prayed that the believers would begin to understand just how passionately God loves them. His love for us is so cosmically enormous that our minds will never comprehend its dimensions. Are you filled to the measure with the fullness of God, or are you running on empty and searching for something to fill your empty spaces?

When you feel completely enveloped in God's huge love for you, you'll trust Him and fully experience His presence in your life. And because of this you'll be able to love others.

God, fill me with Your fullness so I can love. Amen.

God Is for You

With God on our side like this, how can we lose? If God didn't hesitate to put everything on the line for us, embracing our condition and exposing himself to the worst by sending his own Son, is there anything else he wouldn't gladly and freely do for us? And who would dare tangle with God by messing with one of God's chosen? Who would dare even to point a finger? The One who died for us—who was raised to life for us!—is in the presence of God at this very moment sticking up for us. Do you think anyone is going to be able to drive a wedge between us and Christ's love for us? There is no way! Not trouble, not hard times, not hatred, not hunger, not homelessness, not bullying threats, not backstabbing, not even the worst sins listed in Scripture. . . . None of this fazes us because Jesus loves us. I'm absolutely convinced that nothing—nothing living or dead, angelic or demonic, today or tomorrow, high or low, thinkable or unthinkable—absolutely nothing can get between us and God's love because of the way that Jesus our Master has embraced us.

ROMANS 8:31–39 MSG

Praise Jesus! None of the things that come against us today—not our failures, not our feelings, not even death!—will keep Him from loving us. Live loved today!

God, thank You for Your matchless love. Even death will merely usher me into Your waiting embrace. Amen.

He Is Enough

"Were not the Cushites and Libyans a mighty army with great numbers of chariots and horsemen? Yet when you relied on the LORD, he delivered them into your hand. For the eyes of the LORD range throughout the earth to strengthen those whose hearts are fully committed to him."

2 CHRONICLES 16:8–9 NIV

Friend, have you come weary to God's table today? Do the tasks before you seem too much for your flagging energy? Are you wondering how to teach your children, help the hurting, or feed the hungry, when you're just not enough?

A little boy long ago may have also believed that his small offering to Jesus probably wouldn't make a big difference. After all there were over five thousand people and all he had was one small lunch—two fish and five loaves. But instead of holding back what seemed insignificant in the face of such great need, he gave what he had to Jesus.

Jesus promised that His load is light and His burden easy. Whatever you're facing that seems too much for your strength, give Him your hands for the work. Bring Him your fish and bread, and trust Him for the increase. St. Jerome said to cease striving: "It is ours to. . .offer what we can, His to fulfil [sic] what we cannot perform."[11]

Lord, give me the strength to remain faithful.
I offer to You what little I have. Amen.

---

[11] St. Jerome, *Against the Pelagians* (Aeterna Press, 2016), 44.

Confident Hope

What is faith? It is the confident assurance that something we want is going to happen. It is the certainty that what we hope for is waiting for us, even though we cannot see it up ahead.

HEBREWS 11:1 TLB

What is the most significant thing about you? Is it your integrity? The balance in your bank account? Your family connections? A. W. Tozer wrote, "What comes into our minds when we think about God is the most important thing about us."[12]

What things do you believe about God? Do you believe that He tells the truth? Do you believe He is reliable? Good? Just? It's vitally important to spend some time evaluating just exactly what you believe about His character because your beliefs are the lens through which you see life. The deeper your understanding of His goodness and strength and wisdom, the better you will rightly interpret both your battles and your blessings—and His ultimate purpose for your life.

If you believe that life is short, that eternity is long, and that God is good even though life is hard, you'll learn the value of perseverance and the power of God's promises. With the knowledge of God's goodness in front of you, you can live with your eyes on a reality you can't yet see.

God, I believe in Your goodness and truth. I believe that everything You have promised us will happen just like You said. I believe that a fantastic eternity with You awaits! Amen.

---

[12] A. W. Tozer, *The Knowledge of the Holy* (New York: HarperCollins, 1961), 1.

Step Out

Don't become so well-adjusted to your culture that you fit into it without even thinking. Instead, fix your attention on God. You'll be changed from the inside out. Readily recognize what he wants from you, and quickly respond to it. Unlike the culture around you, always dragging you down to its level of immaturity, God brings the best out of you, develops well-formed maturity in you.

ROMANS 12:2 MSG

Conform. Fit in. Don't rock the boat. We spend a lot of effort trying to gain acceptance by a society that has largely rejected God. What if we decided to forget being loved by the world and ran after His love, His acceptance, and His pleasure. What would happen if we lived a radical faith of following Jesus, no matter what He asked?

Peter walked on water when he accepted Jesus' invitation to "Come." What if Jesus asked you not to merely rock the world's comfortable boat, but to step out of it. Would you respond to His leading? Sure, Peter sank a little when he took his eyes off Jesus for a moment, but then he cried out to Jesus immediately. And Jesus immediately reached out to him. If you waver in the radical life of a disciple, call out, "Jesus, I need Your help right now!" He's got you. Just like He always has. And through His supernatural power you can live His best for you.

Lord, give me courage and faith to step out onto the water with You, to radically follow Your leading. Amen.

A Helper

"But the Helper, the Holy Spirit, whom the Father will send in my name, he will teach you all things and bring to your remembrance all that I have said to you."

JOHN 14:26 ESV

How many times have you wished to clone yourself? It's not that we want a copy of ourselves walking around in the world; it's that we need help sometimes. Life can be so overwhelming. There are so many details to straighten out and schedules to keep, not to mention to-do lists that never seem to end no matter how many boxes we check off.

God probably won't clone you, but that doesn't mean He left us without help. After Jesus rose from the dead, it was time for Him to return to heaven to be with the Father. He told His disciples that He was going to get an amazing place ready for them, for us.

It's always hard to lose a friend though. And Jesus said that when He was gone God would send them a powerful helper—the Holy Spirit. As believers, His Spirit also dwells in us. When you're wishing there were two of you to tackle your troubles, remember you've got a Friend. The Holy Spirit knows the answers to all of your questions about living God's plans for you.

Holy Spirit, I need help today. Fill me with Your supernatural power to resist temptations and please God with my actions. Amen.

Live What You Believe

All Scripture is breathed out by God and profitable for teaching,
for reproof, for correction, and for training in righteousness, that
the man of God may be complete, equipped for every good work.
2 TIMOTHY 3:16–17 ESV

It's been asked, "If you were on trial for being a Christian, would there be enough evidence to convict you?" What if I sat in the courtroom during my own trial? Would the evidence presented lead the jury to conclude beyond a reasonable doubt that I love Jesus?

Sure, I go to church and read my Bible. I say that Jesus is my Lord, but what really happens when life hits me head-on? When my kids exhaust me? When the line at the grocery store is too long, or when I lose my keys when I'm already late? Do I resist my flesh, or do I lash out in anger? What if the prosecutor produced eyewitnesses to my impatience or video footage of my less-than-loving words?

As I reflect on some of my behavior, I'm even more grateful for God's mercy. But my life is also the proof of what I really believe. And I want my life to offer solid evidence that I follow after Jesus. Don't you?

Lord, use my time in Your Word to prepare me for the day
ahead. Do life with me today. Help me to resist sin—to do
Your will and not mine in each moment of this day. Amen.

The Right Pursuits

Flee youthful passions and pursue righteousness, faith, love, and peace, along with those who call on the Lord from a pure heart. Have nothing to do with foolish, ignorant controversies; you know that they breed quarrels. And the Lord's servant must not be quarrelsome but kind to everyone, able to teach, patiently enduring evil, correcting his opponents with gentleness.

2 TIMOTHY 2:22–25 ESV

The birds warble their welcome as the first blush of dawn colors the sky. Today is a brand-new day! The morning always feels clean and full of promise because it hasn't yet been blotted by mistakes, poor attitudes, and sins. We're free to choose what things we're going to welcome into our life and what things we're going to turn away from.

What have you been pursuing recently? We pursue many things for even more reasons. We chase down fitness one mile at a time. We sprint after entertainment and pleasurable activities. Some of us run after fame, wealth, enlightenment, or knowledge.

But what about righteousness? Have you planned to please God today? Have you set right living, faith, love, and peace before you and run toward those goals intentionally? If you haven't, there's great news. Today is a fresh start! Don't pursue empty endeavors that lead to spiritual death. You won't be filled by running after other things. God is the only One who can fill you up with life and joy.

Lord, help me turn away from sin today
and pursue righteousness. Amen.

God Is Good

Open your mouth and taste, open your eyes and see—
how good GOD is. Blessed are you who run to him.
PSALM 34:8 MSG

Do you believe that God is good? Scripture invites us to taste and see that the Lord is good. Just as we put a new food gingerly on our tongue and test its flavor, God invites us to come to Him and taste the sweet flavor of His goodness. Put your trust in His promises, and see if He doesn't change your life. Look for His workings around you, and see how your perspective alters.

God is pure, unadulterated goodness. Yes, tragic and terrible things have happened on this earth, but God is still patiently working out His plan so that each one of us might be saved. Hardships may come in this world, but all His promises will be kept—though some not until we reach heaven.

Take His nail-scarred hand, and trust in His ability to work out the rough places in your eternal favor. Trust in His far-reaching gaze that sees both the beginning and the end. If His intentions for us were shaded by anything less than utter goodness, He would not have sent His precious Son into our war-torn world to save us.

Test His flavor today. Savor His love and the beauty of His plan. You will experience His exquisite goodness.

God, You are the only One who is truly good. I trust
You with my present and my future. Amen.

Love Never Ends

If I speak in the tongues of men and of angels, but have not love, I am a noisy gong or a clanging cymbal. And if I have prophetic powers, and understand all mysteries and all knowledge, and if I have all faith, so as to remove mountains, but have not love, I am nothing. If I give away all I have, and if I deliver up my body to be burned, but have not love, I gain nothing. Love is patient and kind; love does not envy or boast; it is not arrogant or rude. It does not insist on its own way; it is not irritable or resentful; it does not rejoice at wrongdoing, but rejoices with the truth. Love bears all things, believes all things, hopes all things, endures all things. Love never ends.

1 CORINTHIANS 13:1–8 ESV

We've all patted misty eyes at weddings when the words of 1 Corinthians 13 have perfumed the atmosphere with the paramount power of love. And it *is* the perfect foundation for a solid marriage. But Paul wrote these words not to a blushing bride in white but to the bride of Christ—the Church.

Sometimes we strive to make big gestures for Jesus and neglect the everyday moments. But Paul says you can give your life and all your possessions yet not gain a thing if you fail to love the people around you. Love well today.

Lord, teach me Your love. Show me how to release it during every moment I live. Amen.

Home

Our citizenship is in heaven, and from it we
await a Savior, the Lord Jesus Christ.
PHILIPPIANS 3:20 ESV

What do you love about your home? Is it the comfort of your favorite chair? The way you sink into your own pillow at night? The beauty of furnishings and decor that speak of your personal style? Or maybe it's the security of knowing you are accepted and loved by the people you find there.

As welcoming as these things are, our house isn't truly home for us. Ravi Zacharias said: "Like a child who suddenly stops sobbing when he is clasped in the arms of his mother, such will be the grip of heaven upon our souls."[13] On this earth we're promised trouble. Wars, smooth-talking politicians, a national obsession with overeating on one extreme and the perfect body on the other, the daily grind of living upright in a sin-steeped culture—these things should leave us longing for a different place.

If your only hope lies in this world, you're going to be disappointed. Your soul will remain unsatisfied as you look around for what's missing. But that elusive piece is not of this world. You can find it only in Jesus and His kingdom—a place where Jesus waits to embrace you in love. The place your soul calls home.

Lord, this earth, fallen as it is, is familiar to me.
Help me resist the temptation to cling to this
place. I do long to be at home with You. Amen.

---

[13] Ravi Zacharias, *AZ Quotes*, https://www.azquotes.com/quote/718655.

Becoming Righteous

For our sake he made him to be sin who knew no sin,
so that in him we might become the righteousness of God.
2 CORINTHIANS 5:21 ESV

How do you introduce yourself to others when you meet someone new? What is the thing that defines you? Is it your relationships to others—a wife, a mother? Is it your work—a nurse, a teacher, a homeschool mom? Or maybe it's by your accomplishments—a dancer, a pianist, an author, a recording artist.

It's easy to wrap ourselves in what we do or who we're connected to in order to be known by others, but as a believer you have an even more important identity. Jesus stepped down from His place in glory for a time to live a perfect life and die a perfect sacrifice for our sins in order to restore us—sinful, fallen humans—to the relationship God created us for.

Because of Jesus' blood, God doesn't see a sin-stained human when He looks at you. Jesus died to pay our price. To blot out our sins. To satisfy heaven's wrath. So that we could be adorned in His righteousness before God. No, loved one, He doesn't see your mess ups, wrong motives, or prideful moments; He sees His daughter. And you are dressed in the pure-white borrowed righteousness of Jesus.

Father, thank You for making me Your beloved child.
Not just a sinner You've let in as the black sheep of
the family, but Your precious daughter. Amen.

Living It Up

My God will supply every need of yours according to his riches in glory in Christ Jesus. To our God and Father be glory forever and ever. Amen.

PHILIPPIANS 4:19–20 ESV

Do your prayers sometimes sound like this: "God, today I need. . . Please give me. . . I want. . ."? Does this verse in Philippians mean that we will never go hungry and obtain every desire that flits through our minds? If we are being supplied according to His riches in glory, shouldn't we be living luxuriously? Before you get carried away and max out your credit card or go house shopping for that mansion, let's stop and take a look at the context of Paul's letter.

Paul was sending encouragement and thanks to the Philippian church for their sacrificial giving to support him. He encouraged them that because they had put their faith in action, he was certain that God will take care of them. They gave generously. . .over and over. Has your coffee budget this month exceeded your offering?

Maybe God has not blessed you with worldly wealth, but He will surely supply "every need." And what He has given already is so much more than mere financial assistance. Through His Son, He has supplied the needs of your eternal soul.

Lord, Your Word says that when I give, it will be given to me. I know that when I trust You and give generously to help others, You supply all my needs. Amen.

Known by Our Love

Always be humble and gentle. Be patient with each other,
making allowance for each other's faults because of your love.
EPHESIANS 4:2 NLT

We like to be associated with the things we enjoy. What can people know about you just by looking? Are you a walking billboard for your favorite sport? Is your status as an Ohio State fan emblazoned on your sweatshirt? Does your bucket hat shout your love of fishing? Or maybe your bumper sticker proclaims your affection for your fur kids.

If your life had a logo, whose would it be? Would people see humility or pride? Patience or anger? Love or disinterest? There's a song titled "They Will Know We Are Christians by Our Love." But it seems that too often we are known by our divisions instead of our love, even within the walls of the church. We complain, we accuse, we hold grudges. Instead of making allowances for one another's shortcomings, we judge. Instead of encouraging, we tear down.

But the identifying marker of our Christianity is supposed to be our love. Because of your love, be humble and gentle. Because of your love, be patient. Because of your love, make allowances and bear with one another. After all, we love because of His love. Today, may everyone know whose you are—because of your love.

Father, may Your love pour from me today. When I'm tempted to respond
in a less than loving way, help me hold back my words. Amen.

Future Glory

Yet what we suffer now is nothing compared to the glory he will reveal to us later. For all creation is waiting eagerly for that future day when God will reveal who his children really are.

ROMANS 8:18–19 NLT

A toddler screams out her frustration. Her shoelace is all knotted up, and she cannot sort it out. Tired and emotionally frazzled, she collapses and refuses to budge. Her parents try to urge her forward; they coax and plead. But the shortsighted toddler will not get up—she'd forgotten they were mere steps from the entry gates to Disneyland.

Don't become like this upset little one. Don't lose sight of what you're waiting for. All God's amazing promises to us are "Yes!" But we live in the *not yet.* "All the promises of God find their Yes in him" (2 Corinthians 1:20 ESV). Our timeline doesn't always line up with His. Our perception of time is skewed because we're human, and He's God. If you ask a child to wait for five minutes, the almost guaranteed response is, "But that's sooo long!" And so it is with us.

But if all creation is eagerly waiting for this day, why are we not also on the edge of our seats? Today, focus on what you're waiting for. You're mere steps from the wonder of eternity.

Lord, keep my eyes focused on future glory. Amen.

Do You Trust Him?

You will keep in perfect peace those whose
minds are steadfast, because they trust in you.
ISAIAH 26:3 NIV

Lily positioned the final flower. The wedding cake she'd created was a beautiful, four-tiered confectionary delight crowned with a riot of wildflowers. She checked the cake one last time before leaving. Her heart stuttered when she discovered her top layer splattered across the floor. She hadn't used strong enough supports, and her layers had lost their balance and crashed to their creamy demise.

Building your life on a flimsy foundation won't end well for you either, friend. And your feelings or the world's next self-help bestseller are not stable building ground. The meaning of the Hebrew word for *steadfast* in this verse is "to support or brace, to uphold." If our minds are upheld and supported by the truth of who God really is and our trust in Him, we will experience perfect peace. After all, our beliefs should support us when things are crumbling around us.

Do you trust God? Do you trust Him to know more about your future than you do? Do you trust Him when you're hurting? Do you trust Him when times get tough? Can you trust His absolute goodness and good plans enough to give Him carte blanche over your life? What about the lives of the people you care about?

Beloved, all you have to do today is trust.

Lord, You are God. I trust in Your good plans.
Thank You for enfolding me in peace. Amen.

Salty Speech

*Walk in wisdom toward outsiders, making the best use of the time.
Let your speech always be gracious, seasoned with salt, so that
you may know how you ought to answer each person.*
COLOSSIANS 4:5–6 ESV

We only get one go-round at this production. It's your one life to live, and the reviews (rave or otherwise!) of how you live will echo through your eternity. The curtain is up, the house is full, and it's your line. This is not a dress rehearsal!

Our time here is limited, and the world is watching. Scripture tells us to use wisdom when interacting with unbelievers, treating every moment as precious. Have you ever considered that the words you choose and the example you live could influence the eternal destination of the people around you?

Grace is magnetic. Season your words and deeds generously with it, and others will be attracted to the banquet you've spread before them. Don't cut down, criticize, or judge other people—that's not the job Jesus gave you. He charged you to be salt, a tasty preservative in a dying world.

Be kind and gentle in all you say today, so others will be drawn to God's transformative grace.

*Father, give me wisdom, love, and self-control as I interact with the world.
Let the words that I say and the things that I do lead them to a life
of belonging to You—our good and perfect Father. Amen.*

Transformed by Trials

We are hard pressed on every side, but not crushed; perplexed, but not in despair; persecuted, but not abandoned; struck down, but not destroyed.
2 CORINTHIANS 4:8–9 NIV

Did you know that olives begin as a bitter fruit? Yes, straight off the tree they're absolutely inedible. They're put through quite a lot to transform them into the useful and tasty treat we pop into our mouths. Raw olives must be washed and broken, salted and soaked—and soaked some more. The bitterness must be cured out of them in order to make them edible. And it can be a drawn-out process.

Friend, have you been wounded deeply? Has bitterness set its roots in your soul? Jesus understands wounds. He was laughed at, spat upon, betrayed, and denied. And then He was beaten and pierced. Yes, He understands our tear-stained prayers and hurting places. But being broken wasn't the end of His story. And our brokenness is not the end of ours either. Scripture says that we are *not* crushed, *not* in despair, *not* abandoned, and *not* destroyed.

No one wants to experience faith-testing hardships, but God can redeem every moment of our pain to transform us. As we are broken open and exposed to the living water, the bitterness leaches out of our human hearts, and we are made useful for His good purpose.

Father, uphold me on the hard days.
I know that in my brokenness and difficulties,
You're forming a heart ready for service. Amen.

Finding Peace

Do not be anxious about anything, but in everything by prayer and supplication with thanksgiving let your requests be made known to God. And the peace of God, which surpasses all understanding, will guard your hearts and your minds in Christ Jesus.
PHILIPPIANS 4:6–7 ESV

Does anxiety crowd your mind and hijack your thoughts? Do worries creep in and leave you feeling shaken and on edge, waiting for the next piece of terrible news? When we're crouching in dark corners, our minds frazzled with fears, we start to feel alone. And when we feel alone, we begin to despair.

But there is an antidote for Satan's cycle of psychological warfare—thanksgiving. Philippians says that giving thanks results in peace. Unimaginable peace. Restful peace.

The process goes like this. First you need something to be thankful about. So pause and look around, my friend. Find one thing to thank God for. Then thank Him for it. And then find another and thank Him for that too. While you are thanking your Father in heaven, you will begin to see Him moving around you. And suddenly you will realize you are not alone. As you continually thank Him for His blessings, a dawning realization will break upon your mind—God is truly in control. He really does have this! And the peace that surpasses all understanding will wash over your mind.

God, thank You for another day to love You.
Thank You for peace in this place. Amen.

Turn Away from Sin

*Point out anything in me that offends you,
and lead me along the path of everlasting life.*
PSALM 139:24 NLT

Clara slammed the pot onto the stovetop. She couldn't believe her friend said that to her. She dropped some silverware into the dishwasher and shoved the rack back inside. Her kids glanced at her from the living room, and her husband's eyebrow arced into his hairline. She knew she was letting her emotions run wild, but those words stung.

She stomped downstairs to cool off. On her way down, she caught a whiff of something rank, but she didn't stop to investigate. She read scripture and confronted her feelings with the truth, but none of it soothed her bad mood. On her way back up the stairs, Clara realized the recycling bag reeked of rotten food.

She stared at the bag, her nose wrinkling at the putrid odor emanating from its depths—and knew that her heart smelled just as rotten in that moment.

Sin is like a fast-spreading cancer to our hearts. God doesn't want you to cover it up and pretend it won't kill you. He wants you to acknowledge it, confess it, and turn away from it. When your attitude starts to stink, ask God to reveal to you the source of your offending behavior.

Lord, show me when my actions disappoint You. Forgive me for sinning against You, and teach me to live in a way that's pleasing to You. Amen.

Find Space for Him

Many are the plans in the mind of a man,
but it is the purpose of the LORD that will stand.
PROVERBS 19:21 ESV

Charlotte stopped in her daughter's doorway. "Evelynn, for the thousand and first time, shut your drawers!" she called down to the living room. Once again clothes were exploding from the half-open drawers like kittens fighting for freedom from her toddler's tight hugs. "I can't," came the reply. "They don't fit!" *Hmm.* Charlotte realized she hadn't cleaned out her daughter's drawers since the summer before, and now she had a mess on her hands.

Sometimes the day morphs into something that just happens to us, like getting steamrolled. Instead of a faithful life lived on purpose, we're dragged around by our overcrammed schedules. In the end there's not much left for the good things in life, and we come out feeling a bit mauled—and we forget to find the good path God would lead us down under all that activity.

Do you need to plan for a bit more margin in your day? Because if you don't leave free space in your life, how can you expect to be available for God's business of the day? After all, when we see Jesus, I don't think He'll be impressed with the size of our day planners.

Heavenly Father, forgive me for scheduling You right out of my day.
My time belongs to You. Help me to use it wisely. Amen.

Wash Me—Again

*Then one of the elders addressed me, saying, "Who are these,
clothed in white robes, and from where have they come?"
I said to him, "Sir, you know." And he said to me, "These are
the ones coming out of the great tribulation. They have washed
their robes and made them white in the blood of the Lamb."*

REVELATION 7:13–14 ESV

I loathe laundry. Can I get an amen, sister? I'm convinced that if I could off-load this one task to a laundry service, a robot, a trained poodle—anyone but me—my house would sparkle 24-7, my kids would reach their highest potential, and I'd have time to actually drink my coffee while it's still hot, with my feet up while I read my favorite book. Okay, so maybe I wrote myself right out of reality and into fantasy land there, but you get the picture. I really do not like doing laundry. At all. Period.

But let's think about washing for a moment. I used to be a dirty rag in need of a firm scrub. And even though I now belong to God and my grime has been washed away by His blood and I've been declared righteous in His eyes, in this life I still stain myself with selfishness, pride, impatience, and unkind words. I mess up and cause hurt. I have faults. I still need the churning of the Holy Spirit to wake up my conscience and point out where I've got mud on my heart.

Lord, keep washing me and making me more like Jesus. Amen.

Faith Acts

Does merely talking about faith indicate that a person really has it?
For instance, you come upon an old friend dressed in rags and
half-starved and say, "Good morning, friend! Be clothed in Christ!
Be filled with the Holy Spirit!" and walk off without providing so much
as a coat or a cup of soup—where does that get you? Isn't it obvious
that God-talk without God-acts is outrageous nonsense?...
Do you suppose for a minute that you can cut faith and works
in two and not end up with a corpse on your hands?
JAMES 2:14–17, 20 MSG

Scripture says that our faith is pretty worthless unless it kick-starts us into doing—in fact, it says that if we're all talk and no action, our faith is worse than worthless, it's dead.

As a believer in Jesus you're living the most hope-filled, loved life you could ever imagine. God—as in the God *of this universe*—loves you. Yes, He loves flawed, sometimes unfaithful, falling-apart you—with a deep, passionate, and limitless love. He walked out of heaven and died horribly just to fling open the doors of eternal paradise for you. Because you're His.

But what He doesn't want is for you to selfishly hoard this perspective-shattering, world-altering knowledge and go about your business as if it were yesterday's back-page advertisement.

Is your faith alive and thriving in loving action today?

Father, thank You for loving me so completely.
Because I am loved I can love others. Amen.

Fruit of His Labor

*Blessed is everyone who fears the LORD, who walks in his
ways! You shall eat the fruit of the labor of your hands;
you shall be blessed, and it shall be well with you.*

PSALM 128:1–2 ESV

Annabelle swiped a trickle of sweat from her forehead and sat back on her heels, tired but satisfied. Her small garden plot was brimming with produce. She plucked a glossy red cherry tomato and popped it into her mouth. Its sweet juice burst on her tongue. She had spent many hours here on her knees—weeding, pruning, watering, and, most important, talking with her Creator. She had cultivated her precious relationship with the One she belonged to with the same daily dedication that she had poured out to her little garden patch. And now her vegetables were mature and delicious to all who were hungry. Annabelle prayed that her life would be as nourishing to those hungry souls in the world as her homegrown vegetables.

Have you allowed the Holy Spirit to till the ground of your heart and pull out the weeds? The cultivation can be uncomfortable and maybe even painful. But, friend, He will tend to your growth with gentle and loving hands. In the end your life will be a bountiful table set before a world hungering for Him.

*Lord, teach me Your ways. Bless me with growth and
abundant fruit so I can spread hope in this world. Amen.*

Remade

He gives snow like wool;
he scatters frost like ashes.
PSALM 147:16 ESV

The first snowfall of winter covers the land in a still hush. The trampled mud and dirty porches are blanketed in pristine white. The brown, dead leaves still clinging to skeletal limbs and blown into haphazard heaps are now wrapped in white. Like a used canvas recoated and made ready for some new artistic endeavor, the world seems to hold its breath in bated expectation for the new masterpiece.

Before we have Jesus in our world, we're broken and dead, brown and dirty. We can't hope to be any better than we are, so we're left with no hope at all. But then Jesus takes our messy lives and gives us His righteousness to wear. He drapes a robe of white right over that dirty mess of impatience, anger, bitterness, and an endless line of mistakes.

He spoke our world into existence, and now He studies the empty canvas of a new life in Him. He lifts His brush, and with gentle strokes He paints a new picture of love, faithfulness, hope, and forgiveness. The Creator of the world creates a heart like His in you.

Jesus, thank You for covering my shame in the purity of white—
in the undeserved glory of Your righteousness. I belong
to You. Make my heart look like Yours. Amen.

Wait for It

Therefore lift your drooping hands and strengthen your weak knees, and make straight paths for your feet. . . . That no one is. . .unholy like Esau, who sold his birthright for a single meal.

HEBREWS 12:12–13, 16 ESV

Susan sighed as she mentally tallied up the items and came to the same bloated sum printed beside the words *amount due* at the bottom of her hotel bill. She'd been so hungry she'd consumed almost every undersized snack bag and drank two of the sodas from the mini fridge during her stay. Regret crept over her as she remembered how she'd spoiled her evening. Her friends had planned to take her out for a special birthday dinner at her favorite restaurant, but she'd ruined her appetite before leaving the hotel and hadn't enjoyed the briny, fresh taste of her seafood.

Esau also allowed his hunger to lead him into a rash decision. He sold his birthright to his brother for some soup! Talk about overpaying for convenience. Esau's poor choice is a warning to the rest of us not to trade our future inheritance for momentary pleasures. So when you feel weary of doing the right thing, when you've lost your eternal focus, lift your drooping hands and remember Esau! Don't sell out your eternal rewards for a fleeting moment of comfort.

Father, I know what I do here matters. When I'm tempted, help me to think about my eternity. Amen.

Walk Straight in His Purpose

*For this very reason, make every effort to add to your faith goodness;
and to goodness, knowledge; and to knowledge, self-control; and to
self-control, perseverance; and to perseverance, godliness; and to
godliness, mutual affection; and to mutual affection, love. . . . For if you
do these things, you will never stumble, and you will receive a rich
welcome into the eternal kingdom of our Lord and Savior Jesus Christ.*

2 PETER 1:5–7, 10–11 NIV

Kendra's little boy stumbled across the room and plopped down onto the couch. "Matt, did you hurt yourself? Why are you walking like that?" Her son grinned and jumped up from his seat, clearly uninjured. "No, Mama, I'm walking just like Daddy!" Kendra turned away to wipe at her tears. Her son had obviously seen his intoxicated father come in the night before.

Our kids mimic our behavior, sometimes in heartbreaking detail. Likewise, those who are young in their faith are watching our example of what it looks like to follow Jesus.

Believing in Jesus isn't the end of your faith—it's the beginning of a journey. Have you added goodness, knowledge, self-control, perseverance, godliness, and love to your faith? Or are you staggering in sin?

Your children and your children in the faith are watching, so walk upright and turn from sin that they too will learn to walk correctly. Be an overcomer in God's plans for you here, and your welcome into God's kingdom will be rich!

Lord, keep my feet from stumbling. Amen.

Live in Power

Crying out with a loud voice, he said, "What have you
to do with me, Jesus, Son of the Most High God?"
MARK 5:7 ESV

Two demon-possessed men lived among the tombs. Scripture says they were so violent that no one could subdue them or pass that way. But the demons saw Jesus, and they recognized Him immediately: "What have you to do with us, O Son of God? Have you come here to torment us before the time?" (Matthew 8:29 ESV). They begged Jesus to send them into a herd of pigs, and so He did. The townspeople came to see what had happened. They heard how the pigs had flung themselves over a cliff and saw one of the men now clothed and in his right mind. And they were afraid.

They'd just encountered the raw power of Jesus. They pleaded with Jesus to leave their region. "Get out of our town," they said. They were afraid of who Jesus is. They didn't know what to do with Jesus, so they told Him to go.

Have you ever been afraid of having Jesus in your life? You don't know what to do with His power, so you ask Him to leave?

Instead of running from the power of Jesus, embrace the Son of God. Tell Him you long for a real encounter with His power.

Jesus, I give my life over to Your power.
Do with it what You will. Amen.

You Loved Me First

*We love because he first loved us. If anyone says, "I love God,"
and hates his brother, he is a liar; for he who does not love his brother
whom he has seen cannot love God whom he has not seen.*

1 JOHN 4:19–20 ESV

Her heart swelled as her squalling newborn was placed on her chest. Damp, a little bloody, and skin tinged red from the trials of delivery—she'd never seen anything more beautiful than her child at this moment. She'd waited nine long months to finally meet her, and she'd longed for her many years before that. Her doctors said it would never be. But here she was—her precious baby girl.

Beloved, you have a Father in heaven who eagerly anticipated your birth. He lovingly planned out the days of your life at the beginning of time. And He's been waiting for you ever since. He set in motion His great rescue, to send His own Son to die for you, so He'd never have to be parted from you again. He did all of this simply because He loved you first.

Love someone today.

*Heavenly Father, I stand in the light of Your love—love I did
nothing to earn. You just gave it freely. I love You back. Amen.*

He's Here

"I've made myself available to those who haven't bothered to ask. I'm here, ready to be found by those who haven't bothered to look. I kept saying 'I'm here, I'm right here' to a nation that ignored me. I reached out day after day to a people who turned their backs on me, people who make wrong turns, who insist on doing things their own way."

ISAIAH 65:1–2 MSG

The house was too quiet, too still. There were no giggling voices echoing off the walls, no running feet, no jumping and bouncing and yelling with delight. The energy seemed to have been pulled right out of the house along with her children. She longed for a bit of peace, but one day into their weeklong stay with their grandma, she realized that she missed their vibrant presence. She missed their chocolate-smeared smiles and skinny-armed hugs. She missed them. She wanted them back. And a week seemed just too long.

Your heavenly Father longs for you to find Him. He aches for your company. Whether you've sought Him or ignored Him, whether you've messed up, whether you've been hurt or been the source of hurt for others, or whether you've tried to do it all on your own, He's holding out His hand. He's there. . . waiting. . .for you. Will you reach out to Him before it's too late?

Father, thank You for reaching for me, for being present and seeking. Thank You for knocking on my door until I opened it. Amen.

Known

GOD, *investigate my life; get all the facts firsthand. I'm an open book to you; even from a distance, you know what I'm thinking. You know when I leave and when I get back; I'm never out of your sight. You know everything I'm going to say before I start the first sentence. I look behind me and you're there, then up ahead and you're there, too—your reassuring presence, coming and going. This is too much, too wonderful—I can't take it all in!*
PSALM 139:1–6 MSG

Making friends is difficult. The older we get it seems to become even harder. We've been shaped and contoured by our history, and it takes effort and time to be fully known by another. But there's joy in a longtime friend! Someone who has shared your yesterdays and understands those sometimes less-than-likable quirks in your personality. You can speak in shorthand with friends and pick up conversations left off months before as if not a day has passed.

Loved one, do you find yourself in need of a friend, someone who knows both your light and your darkness yet wants you just the same? Someone who understands your history and the varied motivations behind your every thought and action? If you're looking for. . .acceptance, relationship, friendship, and love. . .come to Jesus. He already knows *everything*. And He loves you without condition.

Jesus, thank You for being my friend.
Help me be that kind of friend to others. Amen.

Never Cast Out

"All that the Father gives me will come to me, and whoever comes to me I will never cast out. . . . For this is the will of my Father, that everyone who looks on the Son and believes in him should have eternal life, and I will raise him up on the last day."

JOHN 6:37, 40 ESV

Alison drove home from another disappointing visit with her family. She shook her head in an attempt to clear her mother's hypercritical words from her mind. Her mom didn't like her new hairstyle or her job, her church, or even her shoes. Her dad thought she was too lenient with her kids, and her older sister loved to point out that she was divorced and overweight. No wonder feelings of inadequacy pummeled her after even a brief lunch with them.

Our friends and even our families are not always gentle with our hurts and shortcomings, and they're not always gracious in their welcome. Maybe you've struggled to fit in and never found acceptance. If so, don't despair in your loneliness, because there's hope!

God has a special you-shaped spot in His heart, and your place in His family can't be filled by any other. He loves you as His beloved daughter. Come to Him today. Experience His abundant grace and generous acceptance. He won't turn you away or tear you down, and He is always gentle and kind. He'll take you as you are.

Father, I'm coming home to Your presence.
Your marvelous grace has drawn me in. Amen.

Not Your Own

Or do you not know that your body is a temple of the Holy Spirit
within you, whom you have from God? You are not your own,
for you were bought with a price. So glorify God in your body.

1 CORINTHIANS 6:19–20 ESV

We tend to be a habit-driven bunch. And the habits of sin are so hard to break. Just when we begin to think we've arrived at maturity, we're blindsided by another misstep. Then there are the times when we're not surprised at all to find ourselves repeating a sin—because we considered doing what we knew in our heart was right in God's eyes, but then we knowingly chose to do what we pleased in that moment. Maybe it was snapping at our children, telling that little white lie, or repeating an irresistible tidbit of gossip.

We grieve God when we choose sin over doing what is right, because we are His. We were bought at a staggeringly dear cost—the price was a precious and perfect life.

But where is our gratitude when we fail to change our ways after Jesus paid our impossible debt? Beloved, your body is His temple. You are not your own because you belong to someone greater. Glorify Him today.

Jesus, because of You I have a future of hope instead of despair
and death. Give me strength to resist temptation. Amen.

A Real Gem

She opens her mouth with wisdom,
and the teaching of kindness is on her tongue.
PROVERBS 31:26 ESV

What words will be etched into your tombstone? This may be a distasteful topic for most of us, but what *will* your friends, neighbors, and children remember you for? Somehow the words *rich* and *beautiful* just don't have the same weight of importance in death as we give them in life.

Wise and kind—no matter whether the Proverbs 31 woman encourages you or frustrates you, her legacy is something to emulate. Hold these words in your mind when you speak to others. Allow them to become your filter. Are the words that are about to spring from your lips rooted in wisdom? Are they gossip? Lies? Truth? Sarcasm? Have you spoken in kindness? Or have you been impatient? Rude? Angry?

Bathe your mind in the wisdom and kindness of Jesus through His Word because when you're thinking with His mind, you can leave every conversation guilt-free. If you're not sure whether to let the words you're about to speak slip from your tongue, ask yourself, *Are they wise? Are they kind?* If not, it's best to do a quick rewrite of your dialogue before you open your mouth.

When you're tempted to lead with a cutting comeback, stop. Speak life instead. Speak wisdom and kindness. Your worth will be greater than diamonds.

Lord Jesus, fill my mouth with Your words. Make me more and more like
You so that my words show Your love in all occasions. Amen.

Number Your Days

So teach us to number our days
that we may get a heart of wisdom.
PSALM 90:12 ESV

We all have priorities. Whether we schedule our days and make out to-do lists or let life come at us helter-skelter, our actions reveal our true priorities. Is it more important to you in a pinch to pray or pick up after your kids? To spend time in His Word or scrolling through social media one last time before bed? To attend Sunday morning services or a sporting event? Each choice you make is a unique moment spent, and you can't go back for a do-over.

Psalms reminds us that our days here are few, and you only get this one chance at living—so make it count! Live by God's priorities. Don't lose sight of His plans amid the distractions of life.

What does this look like in today's chaotic, gotta-be-busy world? It means not falling for the illusion that your life will never end. That things will slow down later—after your kids grow up or after you retire. God has plans for you today, in the life you're living now. Tomorrow might be too late. And He promises you a heart of wisdom when you begin to evaluate your priorities on an eternal scale. So live for God, for His glory, and for the increase of His kingdom. Do it today!

Lord, teach me to use my time wisely—for You. Amen.

Hope for the Weary

*"I [fully] satisfy the weary soul, and I replenish
every languishing and sorrowful person."*
JEREMIAH 31:25 AMP

There's no doubt that walking the rutted roads of this life can sap the energy from your soul. Maybe that's why Paul compared our faith journey to a race and a battle. He encouraged the believers with phrases like "fight the good fight" and "finish the race." He knew how exhausting it could be to remain faithful when confronted with our own desires and the temptation of sin day after day.

Sin often looks so much easier. And to the tired soul, easier sure sounds better than fighting our way through emotions and self-centered desires. Easier sounds better than serving. And it certainly sounds better than denying ourselves and hefting a heavy cross to follow Jesus.

Jesus didn't promise us an easy life, but neither did He leave us here on earth alone with our battles to be beaten down by inevitable burnout. Instead He said, "Come to me, all who labor and are heavy laden, and I will give you rest" (Matthew 11:28 ESV).

If you're living in a bleary-eyed fog, anxious and fearful about your tomorrows or if suffering and sorrow sear your heart, your burdens belong to Him. Come. Trust in His goodness. Be replenished.

*Jesus, thank You for restoring my strength and refreshing
my perspective. You patiently provide for all my needs—
physical, emotional, and spiritual. Please help me deal
kindly with others when they too need refreshment. Amen.*

God Does the Work

When the poor and needy seek water, and there is none, and their tongue is parched with thirst, I the LORD will answer them; I the God of Israel will not forsake them. I will open rivers on the bare heights, and fountains in the midst of the valleys. I will make the wilderness a pool of water, and the dry land springs of water. . . . That they may see and know, may consider and understand together, that the hand of the LORD has done this, the Holy One of Israel has created it.

ISAIAH 41:17–18, 20 ESV

Some of us are fixers. If something is wrong, we have a solution. Broken? We've got just the tool to fix it. And maybe our pride is stirred a bit by our savvy ability to whip up a cure or mend everything—from a popped button to a broken relationship.

It often takes a problem we can't fix for us to admit our own limits and learn to trust God. When we're trying to do God's job of holding the universe together, He often seems to step back and let us have a go at it. And then He gently asks, *"Are you finished now?"*

In His wisdom He knows our egos will most likely take credit for His work if He steps in too soon. So He patiently waits until we realize that we need Him, that we're spent and empty. That when all our resources have been used up, God remains.

*Lord, help me to rely on You and
not my own strength. Amen.*

Named

You shall be called by a new name that the mouth of the LORD will give.

ISAIAH 62:2 ESV

Have you ever been lied to? The sting lingers long after the words have faded. It leads us to question things we thought we knew. To doubt—others and ourselves. It shatters our trust. We feel shaky about what we believe.

Have you ever lied to yourself? Sometimes we can't even trust the inner voice we hear. We tell ourselves all sorts of wrong things and call ourselves by many untrue names. But you can find hope in this uncertain world by remembering one thing: our greatest enemy is a liar.

Yep, he's a big, fat fibber. Don't ever forget it. When he tells you that you're unworthy, unwanted, unloved, hopeless, or forgotten, you can look him in the eye and say, "Not true!" If he tells you that your name is Nothing, don't buy it. He's bluffing, beloved.

God has given you a new name. He calls you:

Cherished.

Loved.

Known.

Forgiven.

Accepted.

Beautiful.

He is yours and you are His beloved. You belong to Him.

Father, You have called me Yours. You have renamed me and claimed me. Help me recognize the accusations of Satan for what they are—lies. Help me find my worth in who You created me to be. . .in who You say that I am. Amen.

Scripture Index

OLD TESTAMENT

Genesis
3:9 147
15:4–6 69
16:13 25

Exodus
3:7 104
9:16 20
34:29 58

Leviticus
19:32 82

Numbers
14:3 99

Joshua
6:1–2 117

1 Samuel
17:45–46 52

2 Kings
6:16–17 37

2 Chronicles
16:8–9 152

Esther
4:14 125

Job
34:12 104

Psalms
1:2–3 9
16:5–7 11
19:1, 4 105
24:1–3 66
31:7 104
34:8 158
39:4, 6–7 45
46:1–2, 7 141
46:10–11 92
50:1–3 136
51:10 128
56:8 31
56:12–13 91
62:3–6 62
71:14–15 33
73:26–28 109
77:13–20 17
90:12 184
115:3 83
128:1–2 173
139:1–6 180
139:11–12 147
139:17 98
139:24 169
147:16 174

Proverbs
3:5–6 49
19:21 170
23:7 98
31:26 183

Ecclesiastes
3:11 19

Isaiah
25:8 103
26:3 165
28:16 52
40:25–26 64
40:29–31 90
41:10 24
41:17–18, 20 186
43:1–4 8
43:4 131
46:9–10 68
55:11 118
62:2 187
63:9 104
65:1–2 179

Jeremiah
29:5–7 13
29:11 . . . . 13, 34
31:25 185
31:33–34 121

Hosea
2:14–15 61

Jonah
1:3 106

Micah
6:8 87

Zephaniah
3:15–17 95
3:17 111

NEW TESTAMENT

Matthew
4:4 142
5:3 120
5:7 57
5:9 129
5:41 41
6:25–27 71
8:29 177
10:28 139
10:29 139
10:31–32 139
11:28 185
11:28–30 113
14:28–29 67
21:42, 44 52
25:24–30 72

Mark
5:7 177
10:43–45 60
11:25 130
14:36 51

Luke
1:77–79 48
6:35–36 138
8:42–44 55
9:48 144
10:19 132
13:34 56
15:18–20 53
22:41–43 10
23:34 130
24:5–6 . . . . 81, 137

John
4:13–14 46
6:37, 40 181

6:37–39 78
6:48–51 65
10:17–18 135
10:27 133
13:35. 145
14:2–4. 70
14:26 155
14:27. 80
15:9–10. 27
15:10 27
16:33. 101
18:37. 100
21:17 74

Acts
17:26–28. 77

Romans
1:20 79
5:8–10 39
6:11 137
8:1–2. 29
8:5 121
8:18–19 164
8:26–28 108
8:31–39. 151
8:37 132
12:1 38
12:2. 154
12:18 106

1 Corinthians
1:27–29. 148
3:3 146
6:11 88
6:19–20 182
13:1–8 159
15:52–53. 96

2 Corinthians
1:20 164
1:20–22 63
2:11 42
2:14–15 116
2:14–16 102
3:3 122
3:16–17 121
3:16–18 123
4:8–9 167
4:16–18 35
5:6–9 73
5:17–19 18
5:21. 161
9:8–11. 126
10:4–5 86
12:2–4, 7. 120
12:9. . . . . 12, 119

Galatians
3:26–27, 29 22
6:7–8 110
6:8–10 107

Ephesians
1:4–6, 9. 7
1:11–12 15
2:6–9 76
3:17–19 150
4:1–3. 129
4:2 163
4:22–24 54
5:1–2. 26

Philippians
1:6. 123
1:20 43
3:18–19 112
3:20 160
3:20–21 23

3:21 96
4:4 114
4:6–7 168
4:8 98
4:11–12 114
4:13 114
4:19 115
4:19–20 162

Colossians
3:12–13 75
3:23–24 85
4:2 97
4:5–6 166

1 Thessalonians
5:11 89

1 Timothy
4:15 146

2 Timothy
2:22 84
2:22–25 157
3:16–17 156

Titus
2:11–14 50
3:4–6 124

Hebrews
4:16 123
6:1 146
9:28 112
10:19–23 134
10:30 130
11:1 153
11:16 32
12:5–7, 10–11 36

12:12–13, 16 .175
13:20–21 59

James
1:5–6 93
1:17–18 21
1:19 149
1:22–25 127
2:14–17, 20 .172
2:15–17 145

1 Peter
2:9–10 14
3:3–4 130
4:12–13 114
5:7 44
5:8 47

2 Peter
1:5–7, 10–11 .176

1 John
2:4–6 94
4:19–20 178
5:19 104

Revelation
1:14–15 140
1:17–18 140
3:11 28
7:13–14 171
21:1–3 16
21:4 . . . . 104, 143
22:1–5 40